365 Quick Christmas Designs

by the

Kooler Design Studio

Bobbie Matela, Managing Editor
Carol Wilson Mansfield, Art Director
Carly Poggemeyer, Editorial Director
Lisa DeLasaux, Jane Cannon Meyers,
    Pam Nichols, Glenda Tucker, and
    Christina Wilson, Editorial Assistants
Patricia C. Galliano and Mary Hernandez,
    Book Design

Cross stitch charts by:
Rick Causee, Mary Hernandez,
Kyle Nichols, Pam Nichols,
Carly Poggemeyer, and
Brent Rathburn.

Photographed models were stitched by:
Linda Causee, Bonnie Chancellor,
Barbara Chancy, Jessica Chism,
Betty Curran, Maryann Donovan,
Millie Fortner, Ellen Harnden,
Sandi Kardack, Janet Kazmer,
Sue McVae, Maxine Meadows,
Jan Orantes, Mary Alice Patsko,
Carly Poggemeyer, Lee Ann Tibbals,
Glenda Tucker, Christina Wilson, and
Nancy Withrow.

Cross stitch designs by: Barbara Baatz,
Linda Gillum, Jorja Hernandez,
Pamela Johnson, and Sandy Orton.

For a full-color catalog including books of cross stitch designs, write to:

American School of Needlework®
Consumer Division
1455 Linda Vista Drive
San Marcos, CA 92069

or visit us at **www.asnpub.com**

For information about our cross stitch magazine, books, patterns and kits write to:

The Needlecraft Shop®
23 Old Pecan Road
Big Sandy, TX 75755

or visit us at **www.NeedlecraftShop.com**

*Our thanks to Coats & Clark, Charles Craft, Zweigart, Crafter's Pride, Country Wire
Yarn Tree and Westex Corp. for supplying materials for use in this book.*

KOOLER
DESIGN
STUDIO

Introduction

Make your holidays warm-hearted and festive with cross-stitched Christmas gifts and decorations personally made by you.

Cross stitch has become a classic needlework craft, enjoyed for its versatility, portability and artistic expression. As you browse through the pages of this book, you will be amazed at the range of designs—from whimsical to beautifully realistic. You'll find every theme imaginable—lots of Santas, snowmen, angels, elves, edible goodies and even the twelve days of Christmas.

We have shown all 365 designs stitched on an array of useful and gift-able products available to stitchers. Many of our favorites have been arranged and framed for hanging. Recreate the projects as we've shown or use our **365 Quick Christmas Designs** for your own holiday creations and celebrations.

Table of Contents

Bordered in a delicate snowflake design, this
sampler of snow people and friends will make your
home bright and cheerful.

1

Design size: 34 wide x 28 high

	Anchor	DMC
▫	1	blanc
▨	334	606
▨	225	702
▫	1031	3753
▫	367	738
■	403	310

French Knots: 403
Backstitch:
227/701—bear's collar stripes
351/400—snowman's arms, bear
   (except nose)
403—wheels, string, knob on string, noses,
   snowman mouth, vest closures
236/3799—remaining outlines

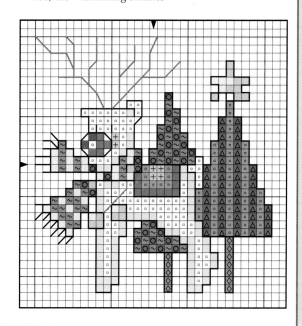

2

Design size: 34 wide x 34 high

	Anchor	DMC
▫	1	blanc
♡	73	963
▫	40	956
▨	46	666
▨	20	815
⌃	314	741
▫	226	703
▨	229	910
▫	1031	3753
~	167	519
△	168	3810
▫	90	554
▨	98	553
■	403	310

Backstitch:
351/400—arms
403—eyes, buttons, hat, boots
401/413—remaining outlines

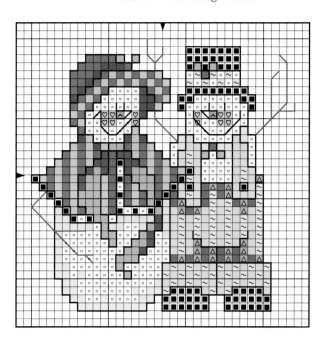

3

Design size: 31 wide x 32 high

	Anchor	DMC
▫	1	blanc
+	73	963
▨	46	666
▨	20	815
▫	301	744
▫	303	742
▫	265	3347
△	267	469
~	875	3813
◎	877	3815
▫	1031	3753
◇	1048	3776

Backstitch:
46—bell string
351/400—antlers
403/310—eyes
401/413—remaining outlines

4

Design size: 33 wide x 33 high

Anchor	DMC
1	blanc
46	666
314	741
265	3347
226	703
1031	3753
137	798
167	519
168	3810

Straight Stitch (scarf fringe): 46
Backstitch:
403/310—eyes
401/413—remaining outlines

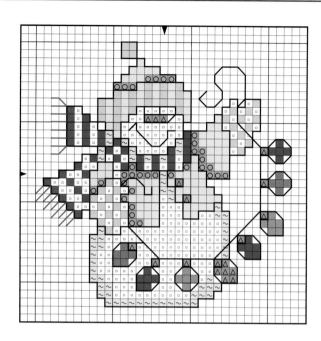

5

Design size: 32 wide x 34 high

Anchor	DMC
1	blanc
73	963
46	666
314	741
226	703
98	553
1047	402
1048	3776
403	310

Backstitch:
351/400—arms
403—eyes, bag trim, legs, shoes
401/413—remaining outlines

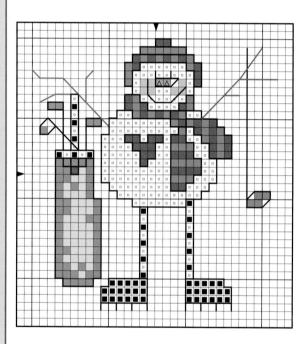

6

Design size: 25 wide x 31 high

Anchor	DMC
1	blanc
46	666
314	741
226	703
1031	3753
167	519
168	3810
90	554
98	553
1048	3776
403	310

Backstitch:
401/413—hat, scarf, cane, tree
403—penguin

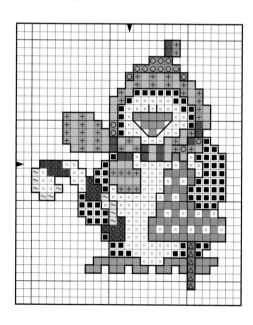

7

Design size: 25 wide x 32 high

	Anchor	DMC
□	1	blanc
■	46	666
▫	303	742
	226	703
	137	798
	1047	402
O	1048	3776
	374	420
■	403	310

French Knots: 401/413
Backstitch:
403—hooves, eye
401—remaining outlines

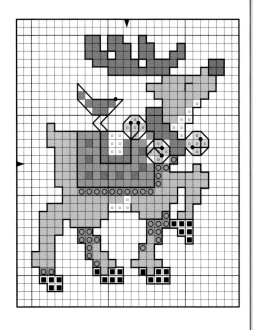

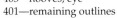

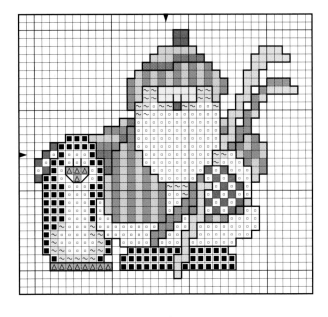

8

Design size: 34 wide x 31 high

	Anchor	DMC
□	1	blanc
	46	666
☐	1012	754
△	314	741
	226	703
~	1031	3753
	130	809
	137	798
	1047	402
	1048	3776
■	403	310

Backstitch:
403—penguin, eyes, boots
401/413—remaining outlines

9

Design size: 28 wide x 33 high

	Anchor	DMC
□	1	blanc
♡	73	963
	46	666
	314	741
	265	3347
◇	226	703
	229	910
	167	519
+	168	3810
△	130	809
~	90	554
	98	553
O	1048	3776
■	403	310

French Knot: 401/413
Backstitch:
403—house hole, eyes, jacket trim
401—remaining outlines

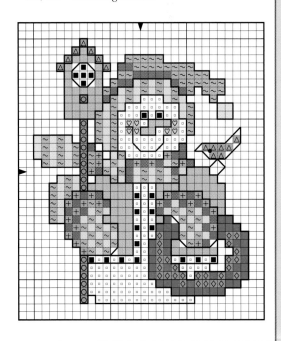

Each day is depicted on a charming ornament for your tree or to give to others. From the three French hens to the ten lords-a-leaping, these ornaments bring a classic Christmas carol to life.

10

Design size: 28 wide x 28 high

Anchor	DMC
1	blanc
46	666
311	3827
301	744
226	703
1001	976
355	975
234	762
403	310

French Knot: 403
Backstitch:
20/815—"1"
229/910—leaves
137/798—remaining lettering
355—pear, leaf stem
400/317—partridge

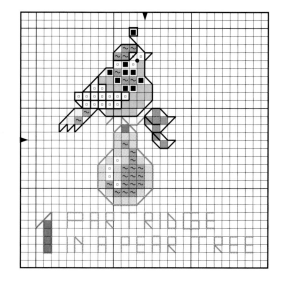

11

Design size: 17 wide x 18 high

Anchor	DMC
1	blanc
46	666
361	738
1001	976
234	762
400	317

French Knots: 403/310
Backstitch:
20/815—"2," heart
137/798—remaining lettering
400—doves

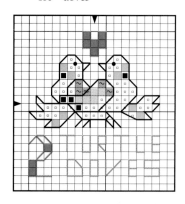

12

Design size: 16 wide x 28 high

Anchor	DMC
1	blanc
75	962
46	666
366	951
368	437

French Knots: 403/310
Backstitch:
20/815—"3"
137/798—remaining lettering
355/975—hens (except combs)
400/317—combs

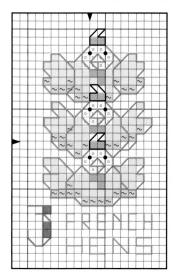

13

Design size: 31 wide x 14 high

Anchor	DMC
46	666
399	318
403	310

Backstitch:
46—neck bands
20/815—"4"
137/798—remaining lettering
403—remaining outlines

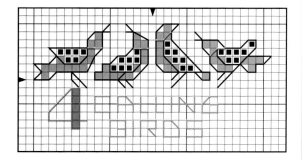

14

Design size: 25 wide x 14 high

	Anchor	DMC
□	1	blanc
~	386	3823
■	46	666
▨	891	676
▨	225	702
▨	129	809

Backstitch:
20/815—"5"
137/798—remaining lettering
355/975—bands
400/317—stones

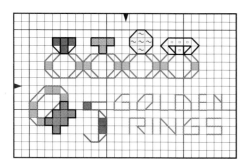

15

Design size: 32 wide x 20 high

	Anchor	DMC
□	1	blanc
□	386	3823
■	46	666
~	302	743
▨	313	742
□	128	800

French Knots: 403/310
Backstitch:
20/815—"6"
137/798—remaining lettering
355/975—bills
400/317—remaining geese, eggs

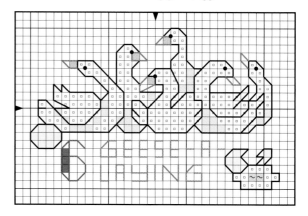

16

Design size: 24 wide x 18 high

	Anchor	DMC
□	1	blanc
■	46	666
▨	313	742
▨	129	809

Backstitch:
20/815—suit stripes, "7"
137/798—remaining lettering, water
355/975—bill
400/317—remaining swan

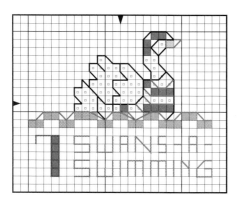

17

Design size: 26 wide x 20 high

	Anchor	DMC
□	1	blanc
■	46	666
□	778	3774
~	301	744
▨	130	809
□	366	951
■	403	310

Backstitch:
46—skirt stripes
20/815—"8"
137/798—remaining lettering, milk
355/975—hair, skin, inside bucket lines
400/317—remaining outlines

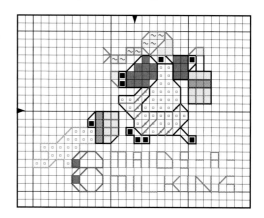

18

Design size: 21 wide x 21 high

Anchor	DMC
1	blanc
46	666
778	3774
225	702
355	975
403	310

Backstitch:
20/815—"9"
228/700—skirt stripes
137/798—remaining lettering
355—skin
400/317—remaining dress, hair

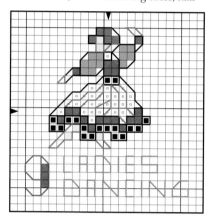

19

Design size: 27 wide x 24 high

Anchor	DMC
1	blanc
46	666
778	3774
225	702
355	975
403	310

Backstitch:
20/815—"10"
137/798—remaining lettering
355—skin
400/317—hair, clothes, shoes

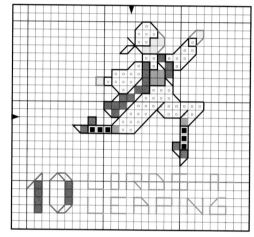

20

Design size: 19 wide x 23 high

Anchor	DMC
46	666
778	3774
302	743
225	702
403	310

Backstitch:
20/815—"11"
137/798—remaining lettering
355/975—horn, face, hand
400/317—clothes
403—hat, notes, boots

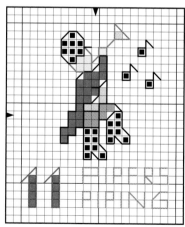

21

Design size: 26 wide x 24 high

Anchor	DMC
1	blanc
46	666
778	3774
302	743
225	702
128	800
130	809
355	975
403	310

French Knots: 403
Backstitch:
20/815—"12"
137/798—remaining lettering
355—hair, face, hands
400/317—top drum edge,
    jacket, straps
403—remaining outlines

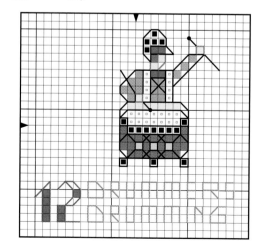

Santa and his buddies relax with hot cocoa and plush
guest towels.

22

Design size: 27 wide x 33 high

	Anchor	DMC
▫	1	blanc
♡	36	3326
▦	334	606
▫	4146	950
~	868	353
	305	743
	131	798
	236	3799
■	403	310

Backstitch:
340/920—skin
403—sunglasses, toy eye & nose
236—remaining outlines

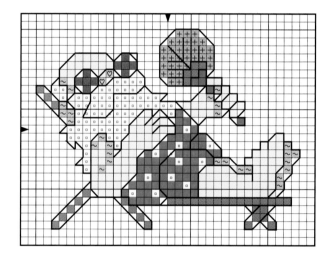

23

Design size: 34 wide x 25 high

	Anchor	DMC
▫	1	blanc
♡	36	3326
▦	334	606
▫	4146	950
~	868	353
+	891	676
	131	798
	236	3799

Backstitch:
340/920—fan (except handle), skin
403/310—sunglasses
236—remaining outlines

24

Design size: 32 wide x 24 high

	Anchor	DMC
◯	50	605
	40	956
	334	606
~	241	966
	226	703
▫	367	738
	369	435
■	403	310

Backstitch:
236/3799—bow, bear (except eyes
    & nose), package
403—eyes, nose

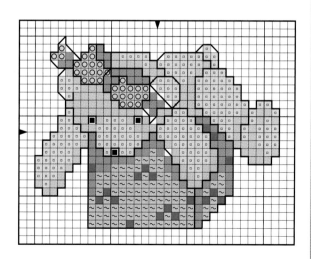

25

Design size: 35 wide x 24 high

Anchor	DMC
1	blanc
36	3326
334	606
47	321
316	970
1002	977
1001	976
241	966
1031	3753
236	3799
403	310

Straight Stitch (whiskers): 403
Backstitch:
923/3818—holly leaves
236—hat, cat (except eyes)
403—eyes

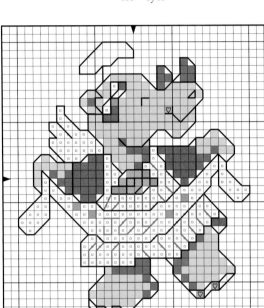

26

Design size: 30 wide x 34 high

Anchor	DMC
1	blanc
50	605
334	606
226	703
108	210
398	415
235	414

Backstitch:
334—lettering, dress stripes
47/321—remaining dress, hair bow
306/783—halo
131/798—wings
236/3799—remaining outlines

27

Design size: 25 wide x 36 high

Anchor	DMC
1	blanc
334	606
86	3608
311	3827
362	437
225	702
227	701
1031	3753
403	310

French Knots: 403
Backstitch:
403—mouths, noses
236/3799—remaining outlines

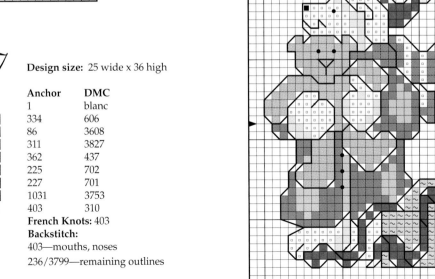

28

Design size: 25 wide x 33 high

Anchor	DMC
1	blanc
334	606
36	3326
225	702
1031	3753
95	3609
97	554
1047	402
1048	3776
403	310

French Knot: 403
Straight Stitch (whiskers): 236/3799
Backstitch:
334—mouse tail
351/400—cat (except eyes, nose, mouth)
403—eyes, nose, mouth
236—remaining outlines

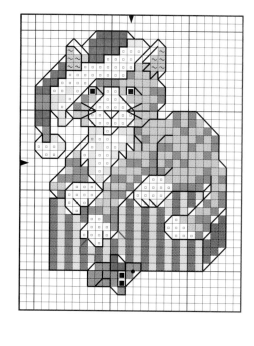

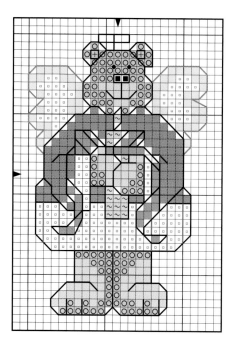

29

Design size: 23 wide x 35 high

Anchor	DMC
1	blanc
73	963
311	3827
225	702
1031	3753
109	209
367	738
369	435
403	310

	Kreinik
gold #4 braid	202HL

French Knots: 403
Backstitch:
334/606—robe stripes
131/798—wings
403—nose, mouth
gold #4 braid—halo
236/3799—remaining outlines

30

Design size: 32 wide x 31 high

Anchor	DMC
1	blanc
334	606
47	321
301	744
891	676
225	702
227	701
398	415
235	414
236	3799

French Knots: 236
Backstitch:
227—scarf fringe
236—remaining outlines

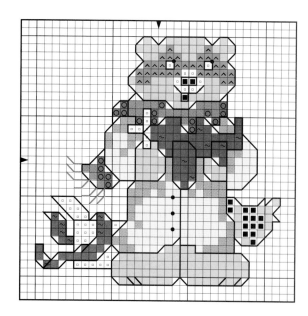

These cheerful designs adorn a photograph album, a
memo pad, and address book for the holiday season.

31

Design size: 27 wide x 33 high

	Anchor	DMC
▫	1	blanc
■	46	666
■	20	815
	316	970
	326	720
	305	743
	303	742
	226	703
	229	910
	231	453
■	403	310

Backstitch:
20—pole stripes, "SANTA"
229—pole stripes, "WELCOME"
403—remaining outlines

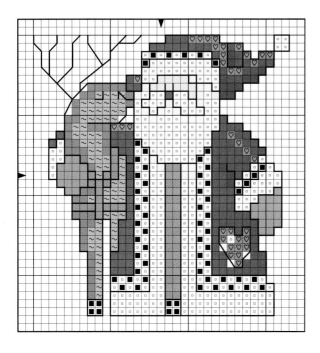

32

Design size: 33 wide x 35 high

	Anchor	DMC
▫	1	blanc
♡	40	956
■	46	666
■	20	815
	1012	754
	265	3347
	1031	3753
	130	809
	98	553
~	1047	402
	1048	3776
■	403	310

Backstitch:
403—eyes, hoof, hat & coat trim
401/413—remaining outlines

33

Design size: 27 wide x 28 high

	Anchor	DMC
▫	1	blanc
	334	606
△	46	666
■	20	815
	4146	950
⌃	9575	3830
	303	742
	240	966
✕	226	703
	229	910
	231	453
■	403	310

Backstitch:
20—berries, candy cane
229—leaves, lettering
355/975—hand
403—remaining outlines

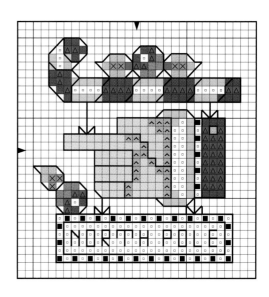

34

Design size: 27 wide x 19 high

	Anchor	DMC
□	1	blanc
~	334	606
	46	666
	20	815
	240	966
✕	226	703
	229	910
■	403	310

French Knots: 403
Backstitch:
46—inner sign border
229—motifs
403—remaining outlines

35

Design size: 26 wide x 28 high

	Anchor	DMC
□	1	blanc
	46	666
	1012	754
~	1031	3753
	130	809
	137	798
	90	554
◉	98	553
■	403	310

Backstitch:
403—eyes, buckle, boots
401/413—remaining outlines

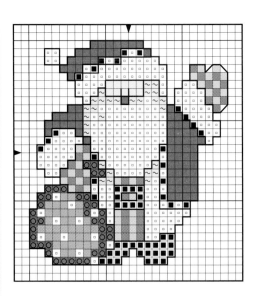

36

Design size: 30 wide x 33 high

	Anchor	DMC
□	1	blanc
♡	334	606
△	46	666
	20	815
	301	744
	306	783
	240	966
~	226	703
	229	910
	1048	3776
✕	340	920
	231	453
■	403	310

French Knot: 403
Backstitch:
22/814—red fruit (except stems)
229—leaves (except stems)
340—all stems, pears
403—remaining outlines

Unique Christmas boots and holiday skates decorate these sparkly fingertip towels.

37

Design size: 23 wide x 25 high

Anchor	DMC
46	666
20	815
303	742
240	966
226	703
229	910
1047	402
1048	3776

Backstitch:
20—berry
229—leaves
403/310—remaining outlines

38

Design size: 27 wide x 26 high

Anchor	DMC		Anchor	DMC
1	blanc		111	553
334	606		1048	3776
46	666			
20	815			
240	966			
226	703			
229	910			
167	519			
168	3810			
108	210			

French Knots: 403/310
Backstitch:
20—berry
229—leaves
169/806—boot top & heel
112/552—remaining boot
403—skate

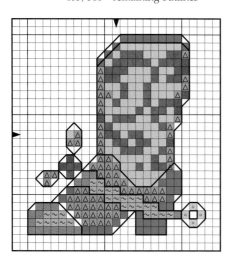

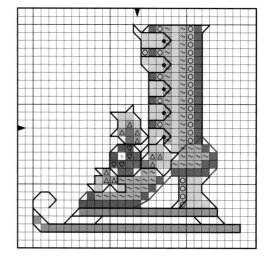

It's beginning to look a lot like Christmas. These simple and
cute vignettes bring out the feeling of Christmas in all of us.

39

Design size: 30 wide x 34 high

Anchor	DMC
1	blanc
46	666
303	742
226	703
137	798
1047	402
1048	3776
351	400
403	310

French Knots: 401/413
Backstitch:
403—eye, platform string
401—remaining outlines

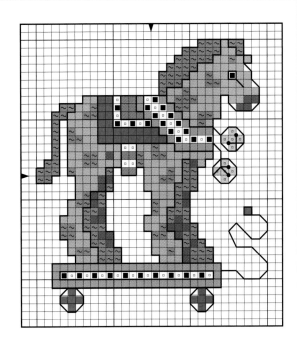

40

Design size: 35 wide x 35 high

Anchor	DMC	French Knots:
1	blanc	46—tree ornaments
40	956	229—lettering
46	666	**Backstitch:**
20	815	20—berry, hearts, nose, hat,
4146	950	suit, candy cane
240	966	229—leaves, lettering, trees
226	703	(except trunks)
229	910	340/920—tree trunks, hands
1048	3776	403—sign, strings, beard, eyes
403	310	

41

Design size: 33 wide x 35 high

Anchor	DMC
1	blanc
46	666
303	742
226	703
1031	3753
130	809
403	310

French Knots: 403
Backstitch:
403—penguin, eye, nose, string
401/413—remaining outlines

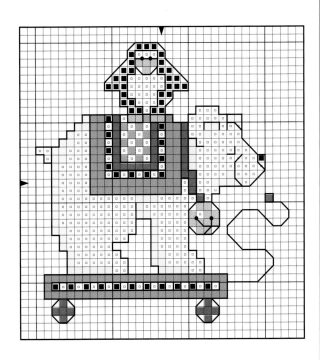

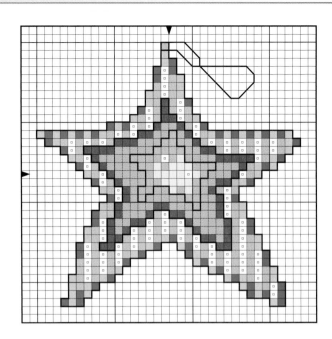

42 **Design size:** 34 wide x 33 high

Anchor	DMC
1	blanc
40	956
46	666
301	744
306	783
226	703
229	910
231	453

Backstitch: 403/310

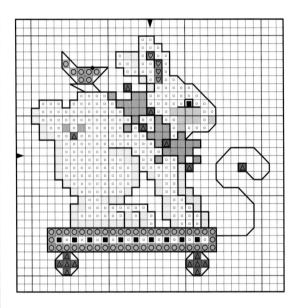

43 **Design size:** 31 wide x 30 high

Anchor	DMC
1	blanc
73	963
40	956
46	666
226	703
1031	3753
130	809
403	310

French Knot: 401/413
Backstitch:
403—eye, string
401—remaining outlines

44 **Design size:** 28 wide x 35 high

Anchor	DMC
1	blanc
40	956
46	666
20	815
316	970
305	743
303	742
240	966
226	703
130	809
142	798
1048	3776
403	310

French Knot: 403
Backstitch:
340/920—star, pole
403—remaining outlines

45

Design size: 33 wide x 32 high

Anchor	DMC
1	blanc
46	666
305	743
303	742
307	783
226	703
229	910
167	519
128	800
109	209
1048	3776
403	310

French Knots:
46—house lights
403—door knob
Backstitch: 403

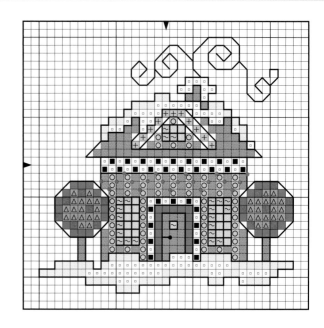

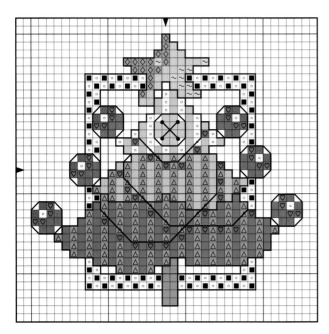

46

Design size: 35 wide x 34 high

Anchor	DMC
1	blanc
334	606
46	666
20	815
316	970
305	743
303	742
240	966
226	703
229	910
1048	3776
403	310

French Knots: 403
Backstitch:
20—ornaments
229—tree (except trunk &
  light strings)
340/920—star, bell outline,
  tree trunk
403—remaining outlines

47

Design size: 35 wide x 34 high

Anchor	DMC
1	blanc
334	606
46	666
305	743
303	742
307	783
226	703
229	910
128	800
130	809
1048	3776
231	453
403	310

French Knot: 403
Backstitch:
46—candy cane stripes
403—remaining outlines

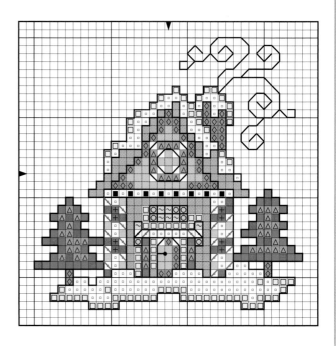

48

Design size: 32 wide x 37 high

	Anchor	DMC
▫	1	blanc
△	73	963
~	46	666
■	20	815
+	303	742
	226	703
	130	809
	1048	3776
	397	3024
^	398	415
■	403	310

French Knots: 401/413

Backstitch:
403—eye, string
401—remaining outlines

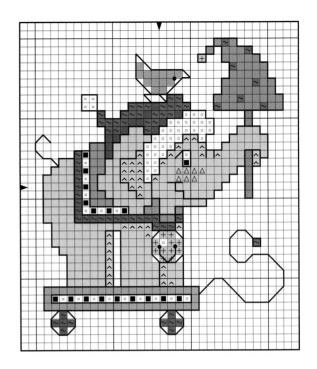

49

Design size: 33 wide x 32 high

	Anchor	DMC
▫	1	blanc
■	46	666
	305	743
~	303	742
	240	966
△	226	703
	229	910
	128	800
○	130	809
	142	798
	375	869
■	403	310

French Knot: 403
Backstitch:
375—tree trunk & branches
403—remaining outlines

50

Design size: 27 wide x 33 high

	Anchor	DMC
▫	1	blanc
^	40	956
	46	666
	20	815
	4146	950
	240	966
~	226	703
	229	910
	128	800
	130	809
✕	167	519
○	1047	402
☆	1048	3776
■	403	310

Backstitch:
132/797—glass
403—remaining outlines

51

Design size: 13 wide x 17 high

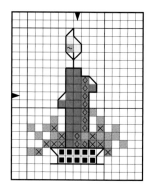

Anchor	DMC
334	606
47	321
329	3340
293	727
242	989
227	701
403	310

Backstitch:
20/815—candle
329—flame
403—wick, holder

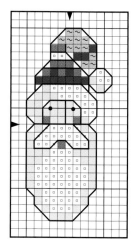

These tiny designs are just right for adding a quick holiday touch to clothes by using waste canvas.

52

Design size: 11 wide x 24 high

Anchor	DMC
1	blanc
893	224
895	223
4146	950
1031	3753
123	820

French Knots: 403/310
Backstitch:
340/920—nose
123—remaining outlines

53

Design size: 16 wide x 19 high

Anchor	DMC
367	738
369	435
403	310

French Knot: 403
Eyelet: 307/783
Backstitch:
227/701—branches
371/434—bear (except nose),
    tree trunk
403—nose

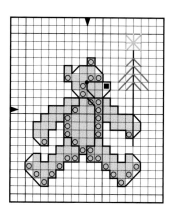

From mistletoe to the star shining over Bethlehem, this
collection of designs reminds us of the many social and
religious aspects of the season.

54

Design size: 33 wide x 35 high

	Anchor	DMC
	31	3708
	33	3706
	19	304
	20	815
	213	504
	261	989
	210	562
	1031	3753
	1033	932
	944	434

Backstitch:
20—ribbon
210—leaves
1034/931—buds
944—stems

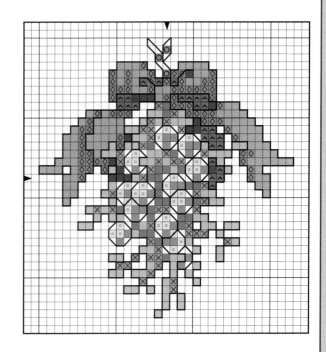

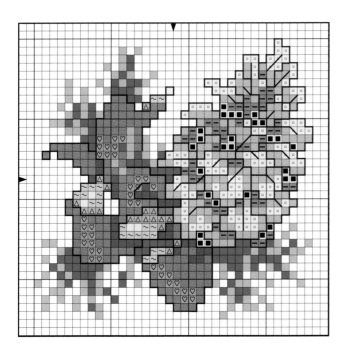

55

Design size: 36 wide x 35 high

	Anchor	DMC	Backstitch:
	885	739	20/815—ribbon
	334	606	1050—pine cone
	47	321	
	328	3341	
	300	745	
	311	3827	
	363	436	
	225	702	
	229	910	
	362	437	
	374	420	
	1050	3781	

56

Design size: 35 wide x 35 high

	Anchor	DMC
	1	blanc
	334	606
	47	321
	19	304
	302	743
	265	3347
	257	905
	246	986
	234	762

Backstitch:
20/815—ribbon
1049/3826—outer wreath edges
246—remaining wreath

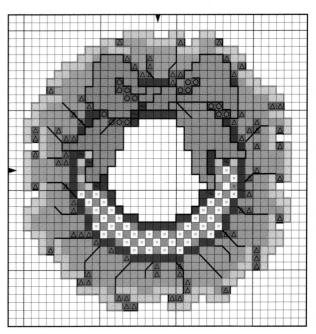

57

Design size: 32 wide x 33 high

	Anchor	DMC
	23	3713
~	31	3708
	35	3801
	20	815
·	253	472
	266	3347
+	267	469
	246	986

Backstitch:
20—flowers, buds
246—leaves, stems
111/553—lettering

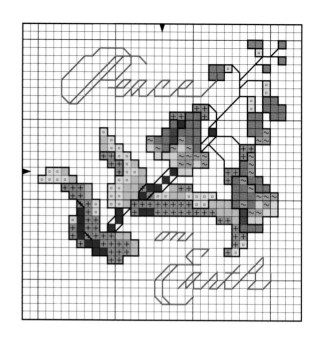

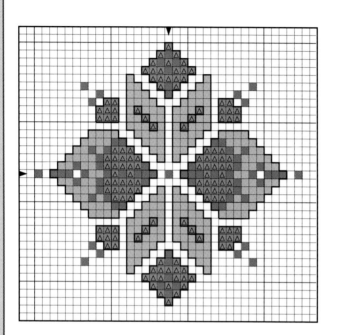

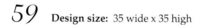

58

Design size: 35 wide x 33 high

	Anchor	DMC
	254	3348
△	266	3347
	210	562

Backstitch: 210

59

Design size: 35 wide x 35 high

	Anchor	DMC
·	1	blanc
	301	744
⊙	305	743
	363	436
+	216	502
	879	500
	1060	3811
~	117	341
	162	517
△	148	312
◇	235	414
■	401	413

		Kreinik
	gold #4 braid	202HL

Eyelet (large star): gold #4 braid
Straight Stitch:
305 (2 strands)—left window
1060 (2 strands)—cross
Backstitch: 1088/838

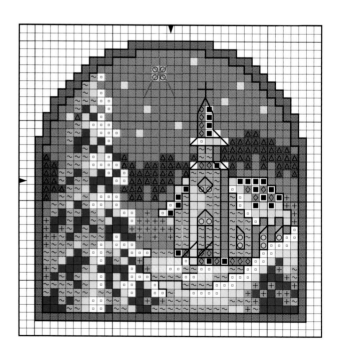

60

Design size: 27 wide x 30 high

Anchor	DMC
334	606
306	783
227	701
358	801

Backstitch: 306 (2 strands)

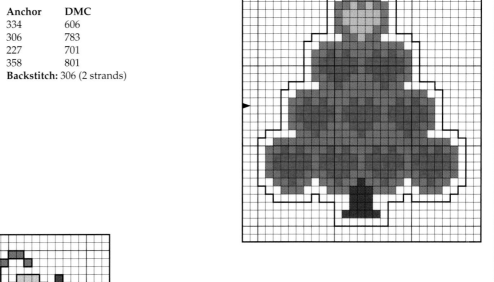

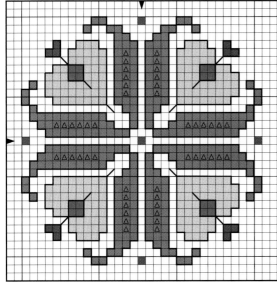

61

Design size: 31 wide x 31 high

Anchor	DMC
334	606
20	815
302	743
267	469
210	562

Backstitch:
20—hearts
210—leaves

62

Design size: 35 wide x 35 high

Anchor	DMC
4146	950
301	744
241	966
216	502
879	500
928	3811
175	809
162	517
148	312
373	3828
375	869
1088	838

	Kreinik
gold #4 braid	202HL

Eyelet(large star): **gold #4 braid**
Backstitch: 1088 (2 strands)
Backstitch: 1088

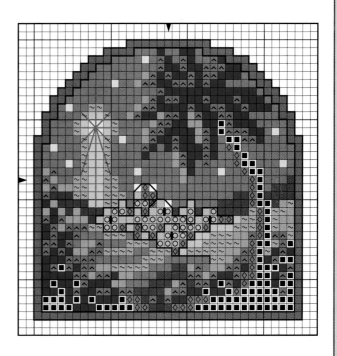

Christmas is also a quiet time to reflect on friends and
family. These images are both festive and serene, helping us
to realize the peacefulness of the season.

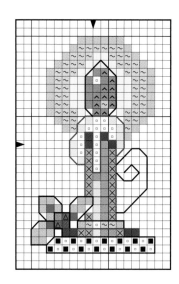

63

Design size: 16 wide x 27 high

	Anchor	DMC		Anchor	DMC
▫	1	blanc	☐	128	800
	334	606		130	809
△	46	666	✕	142	798
	20	815		139	797
∧	316	970	■	403	310
☐	300	745			
~	305	743			
	303	742			
	226	703			
	229	910			

Backstitch:
20—flame, berry, gold portion of base
229—leaves
139—candle, blue portion of base
403—handle, checked base

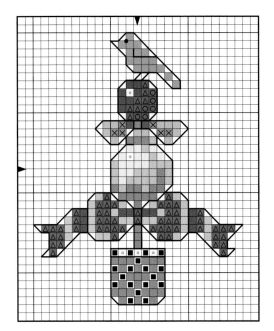

64

Design size: 27 wide x 34 high

	Anchor	DMC
▫	1	blanc
	40	956
⊙	334	606
△	46	666
	20	815
	1048	3776
☐	301	744
	306	783
	240	966
✕	226	703
	229	910
	130	809
■	403	310

French Knot: 403
Backstitch:
20—cherry, bow
229—leaves
340/920—pear, stem, trunk
403—remaining outlines

65

Design size: 31 wide x 34 high

	Anchor	DMC
△	46	666
	20	815
☐	305	743
~	303	742
	316	970
	240	966
✕	226	703
	229	910
∧	1048	3776

Backstitch:
46—strings
20—candles, red portion of base
229—green edges of stand
340/920—flames, vertical pole of stand

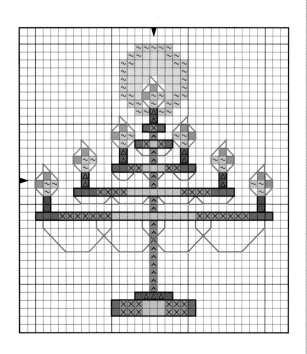

66

Design size: 24 wide x 35 high

	Anchor	DMC
▫	1	blanc
	40	956
	46	666
	20	815
⌃	316	970
~	305	743
	303	742
	226	703
	229	910
	109	209
	1048	3776
✕	340	920
■	403	310

Backstitch:
22/814—red ornaments, bow
229—tree (except trunk)
340—star, tree trunk, pot (except checked borders)
403—pot borders

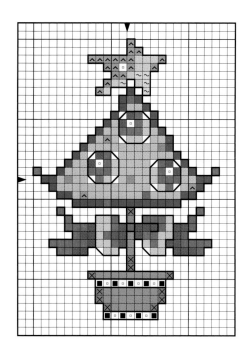

67

Design size: 20 wide x 18 high

	Anchor	DMC
▫	1	blanc
	46	666
◉	20	815
	4146	950
	240	966
◇	226	703
	229	910
	128	800
■	403	310

French Knots: 403
Backstitch: 403

68

Design size: 19 wide x 22 high

	Anchor	DMC
▫	1	blanc
	334	606
	47	321
~	301	744
	302	743
	1031	3753
	131	798
	398	415
■	403	310

French Knot: 403
Backstitch:
227/701—hat stripes
351/400—moon (except eye)
403—eye
236/3799—remaining outlines

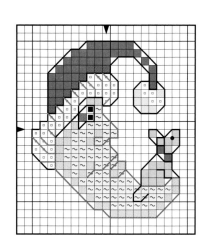

69

Design size: 28 wide x 19 high

	Anchor	DMC
□	1	blanc
~	334	606
	46	666
	20	815
	240	966
	226	703
	128	800
	130	809

Backstitch:
20—berry
229/910—leaves, stem
137/798—bird (except eye & beak)
403/310—eye, beak

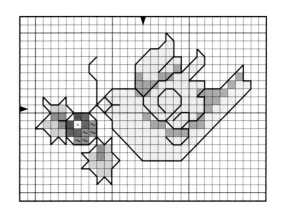

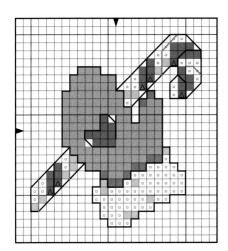

70

Design size: 22 wide x 24 high

	Anchor	DMC
□	1	blanc
	334	606
△	47	321
	265	3347
	210	562
	234	762

Backstitch:
265—candy cane stripes
20/815—remaining candy cane, heart
211/561—mitten (except cuff)
399/318—mitten cuff

71

Design size: 21 wide x 25 high

	Anchor	DMC
□	1	blanc
	46	666
	240	966
	227	701
	234	762
	399	318
■	403	310

French Knots: 403
Backstitch:
46—cup stripes
400/317—remaining outlines

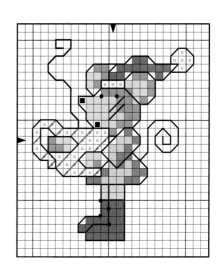

With all of their hearts, these kids are determined to
make this the best Christmas pageant ever.

72

Design size: 23 wide x 31 high

	Anchor	DMC
▫	1	blanc
	1012	754
~	300	745
	311	3827
	1031	3753
△	130	809

	Kreinik
gold #4 braid	202HL

French Knots: 403/310
Backstitch:
76/961—mouth
306/783—sleeve trim
131/798—wings, remaining gown
355/975—skin, nose, hair
gold #4 braid—halo

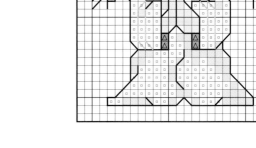

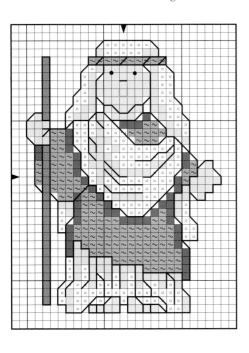

73

Design size: 25 wide x 34 high

	Anchor	DMC
▫	1	blanc
~	334	606
	47	321
	1012	754
	1031	3753
	899	3782

French Knots: 403/310
Backstitch:
76/961—mouth
355/975—skin, nose, staff
403—headband stripes
236/3799—remaining outlines

74

Design size: 25 wide x 31 high

	Anchor	DMC
▫	1	blanc
	1012	754
	302	743
	1031	3753
○	108	210
	109	209
~	1047	402
■	904	640

French Knots:
355/975—baby's eye
403/310—mom's eyes
Backstitch:
76/961—mouth
355—skin, nose, baby's hair
904—mom's hair
236/3799—remaining outlines

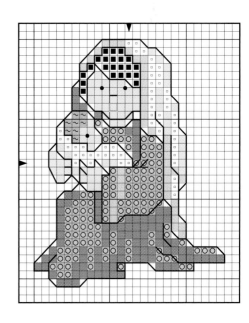

75

Design size: 18 wide x 34 high

Anchor	DMC
1	blanc
1012	754
128	800
130	809
146	798
885	739
347	402
369	435
235	414

French Knots: 403/310

Backstitch:
76/961—mouth
146—sleeve stripes
355/975—clothes, skin, nose, hair
236/3799—lamb, shoes

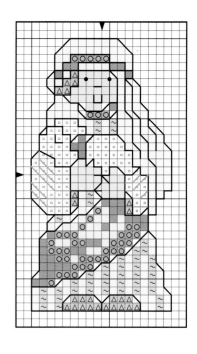

76

Design size: 35 wide x 32 high

Anchor	DMC
1	blanc
1012	754
225	702
227	701
1031	3753
108	210
109	209
367	738
368	437
369	435
235	414
403	310

French Knots: 403
Backstitch:
76/961—mouth
225—sleeve stripes
355/975—headband stripes,
skin, shepherd's nose,
hair
403—lamb's nose
236/3799—remaining
outlines

77

Design size: 34 wide x 29 high

Anchor	DMC
1	blanc
334	606
47	321
891	676
890	729
238	703
881	945
1047	402
398	415
400	317
403	310

Backstitch:
403—eye, mouth, nostril,
inner ear, hoofs
351/400—remaining camel,
saddle
236/3799—remaining outlines

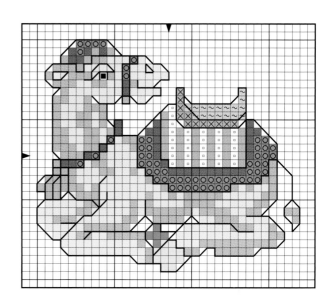

78

Design size: 21 wide x 34 high

	Anchor	DMC
▫	1	blanc
■	334	606
☐	1012	754
~	305	743
⊙	306	783
▨	238	703
▨	130	809
△	131	798
▢	369	435

French Knot: 403/310
Backstitch:
76/961—mouth
334—robe stripes
355/975—hair, skin, nose, crown, scepter
236/3799—remaining outlines

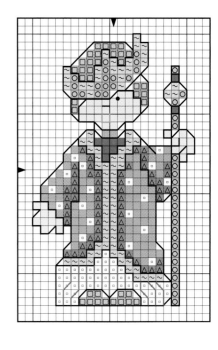

79

Design size: 18 wide x 33 high

	Anchor	DMC
▫	1	blanc
~	75	962
▨	76	961
☐	1012	754
☐	301	744
☐	302	743
☐	1031	3753
▨	96	3609
▨	110	208
■	904	640

French Knots: 403/310
Backstitch:
76—mouth, jewel, box latch
302—robe stripes
355/975—skin, nose
904—hair
236/3799—remaining outlines

80

Design size: 28 wide x 28 high

	Anchor	DMC
▫	1	blanc
■	334	606
☐	1012	754
☐	868	353
☐	305	743
⊙	306	783
☐	253	472
~	225	702
△	227	701
▨	110	208
⊠	369	435
■	403	310

French Knots: 403
Straight Stitch (hair): 355/975
Backstitch:
76/961—mouth
334—bow
355—crown, skin, nose
403—box latch & trim
236/3799—remaining outlines

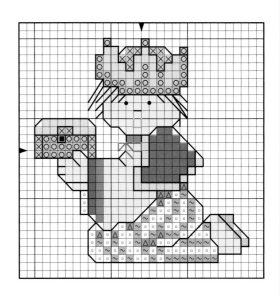

81

Design size: 35 wide x 16 high

Anchor	DMC
334	606
47	321
302	743
307	783
254	3348
257	905

Backstitch:
20/815—ribbons, berries
246/986—leaves
1049/3826—bells

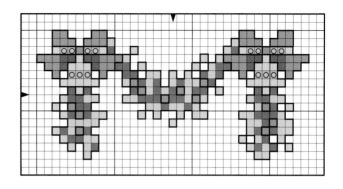

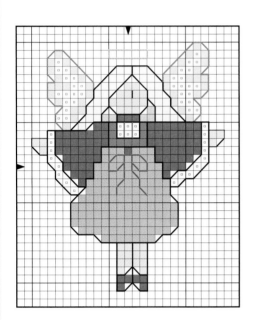

82

Design size: 25 wide x 31 high

Anchor	DMC
1	blanc
334	606
778	3774
300	745
302	743
240	966
227	701
128	800

	Kreinik
gold #4 braid	202HL

Backstitch:
334—bodice stripes, bow
131/798—wings
355/975—hair, nose, skin
400/317—robe, shoes
gold #4 braid—halo

83

Design size: 26 wide x 30 high

Anchor	DMC
1	blanc
334	606
4146	950
868	353
891	676
225	702
367	738
235	414
403	310

French Knots: 403
Backstitch:
47/321—her nose & mouth
355/975—hair, skin, bear (except nose)
403—hat, clothes, box, bear nose

This is what he enjoys the rest of the year!

84

Design size: 26 wide x 28 high

	Anchor	DMC
▫	1	blanc
▨	334	606
□	4146	950
□	1031	3753
~	347	402
■	403	310

French Knots: 403
Backstitch:
334—hat letter, ball stitching, pant stripes
340/920—skin
403—hat bill, belt, shoes
236/3799—remaining outlines

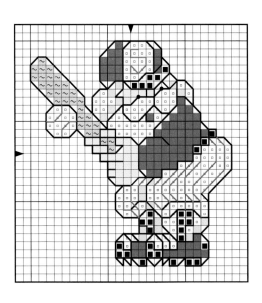

85

Design size: 31 wide x 33 high

	Anchor	DMC
▫	1	blanc
▨	334	606
△	47	321
□	4146	950
~	868	353
▨	306	783
□	1031	3753
+	347	402
▨	355	975
■	403	310

Backstitch:
355—skin
236/3799—helmet, hair, clothes, football
403—belt, eye, shoes

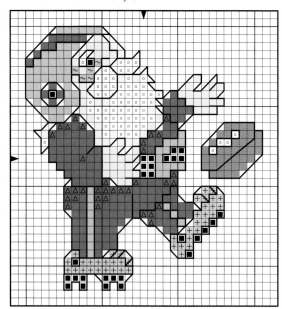

Santa's elves, with their play hard, work hard ethic, are
busy getting ready for the holidays and having fun, too!

86

Design size: 26 wide x 28 high

Anchor	DMC
1	blanc
334	606
1012	754
225	702
368	437

French Knots:
236/3799—eyes
403/310—jacket

Backstitch:
46/666—hat & collar stripes, thread
236—remaining outlines

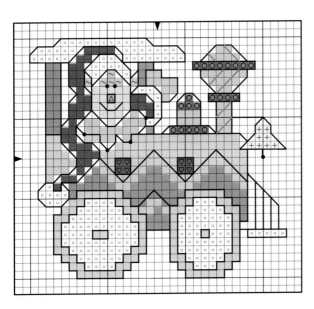

87

Design size: 33 wide x 30 high

Anchor	DMC
1	blanc
334	606
85	3609
778	3774
6	754
8	3824
300	745
311	3827
225	702
227	701
110	208
398	415

French Knots: 236/3799
Backstitch:
227—smokestack stripes
236—remaining outlines

88

Design size: 22 wide x 26 high

Anchor	DMC
1	blanc
334	606
46	666
86	3608
778	3774
6	754
8	3824
301	744
225	702
227	701
131	798
347	402
1048	3776

French Knots:
46—shoes
236/3779—eyes
Backstitch:
46—stocking stripes
227—tree
236—remaining outlines

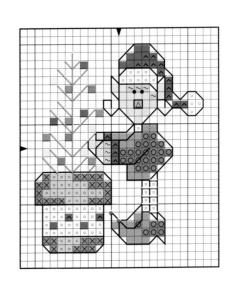

89

Design size: 24 wide x 25 high

Anchor	DMC
1	blanc
46	666
47	321
778	3774
311	3827
313	742
240	966
228	700
1007	3772

French Knots: 403/310

Backstitch:
228—stockings, sleeve cuff
400/317—remaining outlines

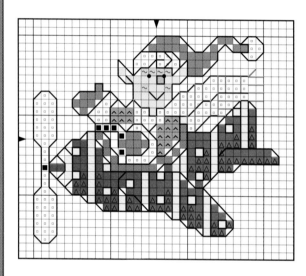

90

Design size: 32 wide x 26 high

Anchor	DMC
1	blanc
334	606
46	666
778	3774
6	754
8	3824
301	744
225	702
227	701
137	798
236	3799

French Knots: 236

Straight Stitch (scarf fringe): 46

Backstitch:
46—scarf stripes
236—remaining outlines

91

Design size: 28 wide x 35 high

Anchor	DMC
1	blanc
334	606
85	3609
778	3774
6	754
8	3824
311	3827
225	702
227	701
137	798

French Knots:
110/208—ribbon
236/3799—eyes

Backstitch:
334—hat & clothes plaid, package stripes
891/676—hair
227—hat & clothes plaid, package stripes
236—remaining outlines

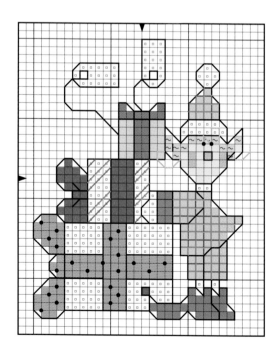

92

Design size: 32 wide x 34 high

Anchor	DMC
1	blanc
26	894
46	666
47	321
778	3774
311	3827
225	702
876	3816

French Knots:
46—bell, shoes
403/310—eyes, buttons

Backstitch:
227/701—bell zigzags & stripes
400/317—remaining outlines

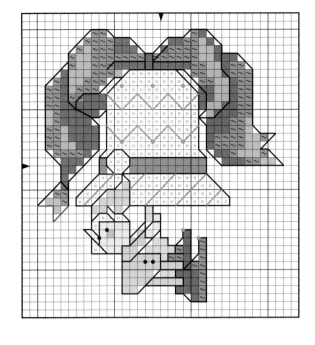

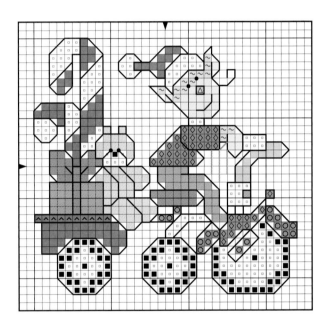

93

Design size: 34 wide x 32 high

Anchor	DMC		Anchor	DMC
1	blanc	◇	227	701
86	3608		137	798
334	606		398	415
46	666	◯	235	414
778	3774	■	236	3799
6	754		**French Knots:** 236	
8	3824		**Straight Stitch** (handle	
361	738		fringe): 137	
225	702		**Backstitch:** 236	

94

Design size: 22 wide x 35 high

Anchor	DMC
1	blanc
334	606
86	3608
778	3774
300	745
311	3827
225	702
227	701
110	208

French Knots:
46/666—balloon
236/3799—eyes, nose

Backstitch:
46—balloon zigzags
227—basket fringe
236—remaining outlines

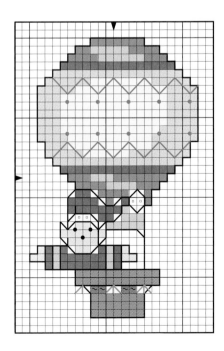

95

Design size: 30 wide x 25 high

Anchor	DMC
1	blanc
46	666
1012	754
225	702
368	437

French Knots: 403/310
Backstitch:
46—front spool thread, stocking
228/700—hat, collar, stocking, & sock stripes;
    back spool thread
236/3799—remaining outlines

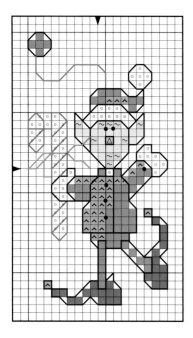

96

Design size: 18 wide x 34 high

Anchor	DMC
1	blanc
46	666
778	3774
6	754
8	3824
225	702
227	701
131	798

French Knots:
227—bow
236/3799—eyes, buttons
Backstitch:
46—candy cane, toy string
227—candy cane bow
236—remaining outlines

97

Design size: 21 wide x 19 high

Anchor	DMC
1	blanc
46	666
891	676
209	913
130	809
131	798

French Knots: 46
Backstitch:
46—candy cane, ornament (except top)
236/3799—remaining outlines

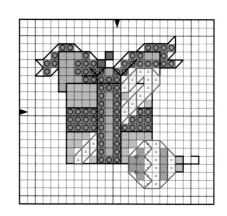

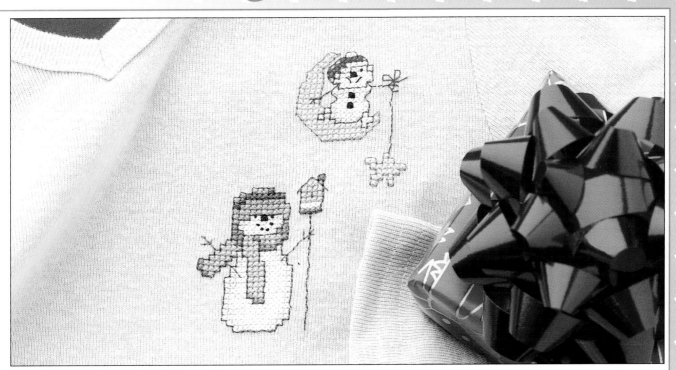

Whether tending a birdhouse or hanging a Christmas star, these snowmen are on the job.

98

Design size: 20 wide x 26 high

	Anchor	DMC
▫	1	blanc
■	334	606
░	311	3827
▫	1031	3753
■	403	310

French Knot: 403
Backstitch:
46/666—string
355/975—moon, star
360/898—arms
403—nose, buttons, mouth
236/3799—remaining outlines

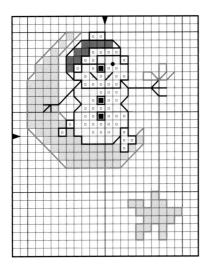

99

Design size: 23 wide x 29 high

	Anchor	DMC
▫	1	blanc
~	894	223
▒	1027	3722
△	859	523
▓	861	520
▫	1031	3753
■	403	310

French Knots: 403
Backstitch:
358/801—arms
403—nose
236/3799—remaining outlines

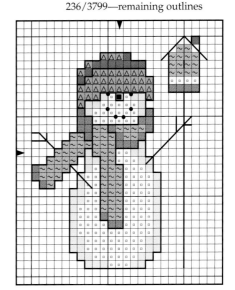

There are carols to be sung, trees to be decorated, wreaths to hang and gifts to wrap—the holidays are a snowman's favorite time of the year.

100

Design size: 22 wide x 34 high

Anchor	DMC
1	blanc
46	666
372	738
885	739
301	744
313	742
875	3813
128	800
131	798
400	317

French Knots: 46
Eyelet (star): 130/809
Backstitch:
46—doorway
210/562—tree, light cord
400—remaining outlines

101

Design size: 35 wide x 31 high

Anchor	DMC
1	blanc
334	606
305	743
225	702
1031	3753
130	809
131	798
369	435

French Knots:
334—doorknob, ornaments
305—ornaments
Eyelets (stars): 131
Backstitch:
227/701—trees
131—snow, main roof
400/317—remaining outlines

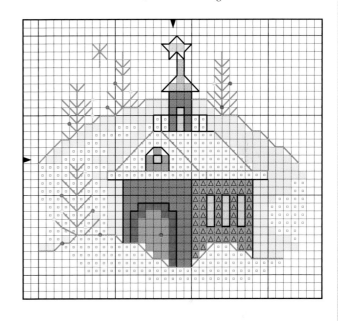

102

Design size: 83 wide x 12 high

Anchor	DMC
334	606
254	3348
266	3347
210	562

Backstitch:
334—berries
254—vines
210—leaves

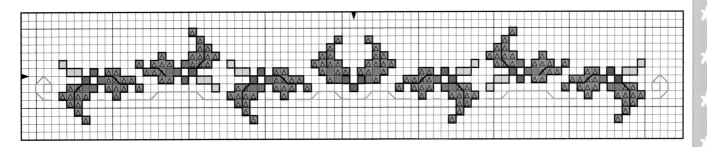

103

Design size: 25 wide x 31 high

Anchor	DMC
1	blanc
46	666
47	321
311	3827
228	700
128	800
403	310

French Knots:
46—berries
403—eyes, buttons
Backstitch:
46—notes, berry
228—scarf fringe
140/3755—snowman (except face), snow
403—face
400/317—remaining outlines

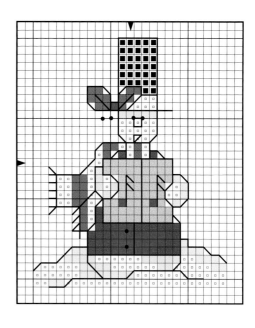

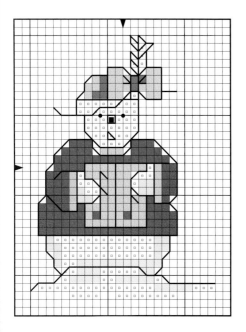

104

Design size: 24 wide x 33 high

Anchor	DMC
1	blanc
46	666
47	321
311	3827
240	966
228	700
128	800
400	317

French Knots: 403/310
Backstitch:
46—notes
140/3755—feather, snowlady (except
    nose & mouth), snow
400—hat, book, sweater
403—nose, mouth

105

Design size: 24 wide x 29 high

Anchor	DMC
1	blanc
46	666
311	3827
240	966
229	910
128	800
403	310

French Knots: 403
Straight Stitch (scarf fringe): 46
Backstitch:
46—note
140/3755—snowman (except nose
    & mouth), snow
400/317—remaining outlines

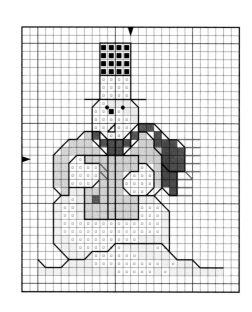

106

Design size: 22 wide x 31 high

	Anchor	DMC
▫	1	blanc
■	46	666
☐	311	3827
■	228	700
☐	128	800
~	130	809
■	941	792

French Knot: 403/310
Straight Stitch (scarf fringe): 46
Backstitch:
46—scarf stripes, red notes
228—branches, green notes
130—snow
400/317—remaining outlines

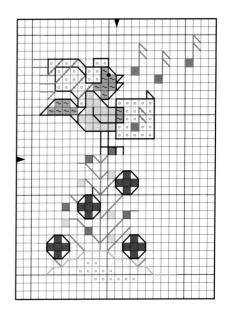

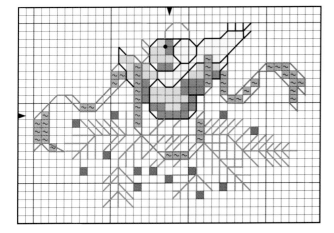

107

Design size: 35 wide x 23 high

	Anchor	DMC
~	46	666
■	47	321
☐	300	745
☐	130	809
■	131	798

French Knot: 403/310
Backstitch:
47—ribbon
302/743—scarf fringe
210/562—branch
355/975—beak, feet
400/317—remaining outlines

108

Design size: 24 wide x 35 high

	Anchor	DMC
▫	1	blanc
☐	26	894
■	46	666
☐	300	745
☐	311	3827
☐	130	809
■	131	798
~	336	758
☐	1048	3776

French Knots: 403/310
Backstitch:
210/562—tree
400/317—remaining outlines

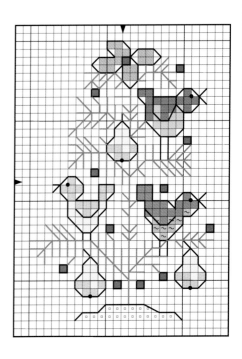

109

Design size: 32 wide x 32 high

	Anchor	DMC
▫	1	blanc
▲	46	666
☐	301	744
~	313	742
+	203	564
▨	876	3816
☐	128	800
▨	96	3609
▨	1047	402
▨	1049	3826
■	236	3799

Eyelets (stars): 130/809
Backstitch:
225/702—gift ribbons
210/562—tree
97/554—gift ribbons
400/317—remaining outlines

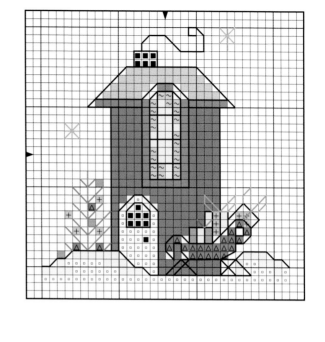

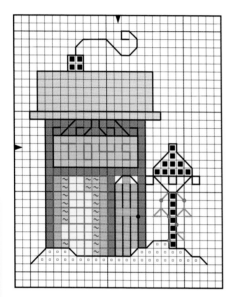

110

Design size: 23 wide x 29 high

	Anchor	DMC
▫	1	blanc
▨	46	666
☐	301	744
~	313	742
▨	876	3816
☐	129	809
☐	368	437
■	236	3799

French Knots:
47/321—berries
236—doorknob
Backstitch:
47—lettering, windows
876—leaves
236—remaining outlines

111

Design size: 27 wide x 35 high

	Anchor	DMC
▫	1	blanc
▨	46	666
☐	301	744
~	313	742
+	206	564
▨	208	563
☐	128	800
☐	336	758
▨	1007	3772
■	400	317

French Knots:
46—nose
403/310—eyes, doorknob
Straight Stitch (scarf fringe): 46
Eyelets (stars): 130/809
Backstitch: 400

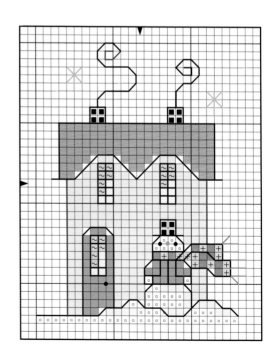

112

Design size: 12 wide x 15 high

	Anchor	DMC
□	1	blanc
▨	361	738
■	403	310

French Knots: 403
Backstitch:
46/666—bone stripes
355/975—dog (except nose)
403—mouth, bone outline

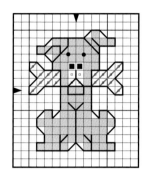

113

Design size: 16 wide x 12 high

	Anchor	DMC
▨	334	606
〰	47	321
□	302	743
□	1043	369
⊠	203	564
△	205	912
▨	211	562

Backstitch:
20/815—gift
302 (2 strands)—ribbon stripes
211—remaining ribbon

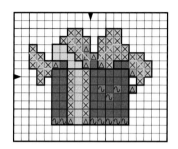

114

Design size: 13 wide x 16 high

	Anchor	DMC
▨	334	606
⊙	47	321
□	302	743
︿	307	783
□	254	3348
▨	257	905
▨	358	801

Backstitch:
20/815—ribbon, ornaments
246/986—tree (except trunk)
358—tree trunk

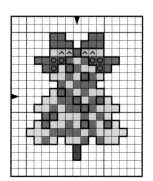

115

Design size: 17 wide x 17 high

	Anchor	DMC
▨	334	606
⊙	47	321
□	302	743
⊠	307	783
□	254	3348
▨	257	905

Backstitch:
20/815—ribbon, berries
246/986—leaves
1049/3826—bell

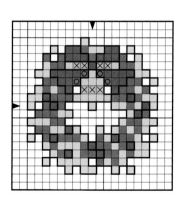

These picture-perfect accessories will give even the
youngest member of the family a joyful smile.

116

Design size: 22 wide x 27 high

	Anchor	DMC
▫	1	blanc
	49	3689
	40	956
△	46	666
	229	910
	397	3024
✕	399	318
■	403	310

French Knots: 403
Backstitch: 403

117

Design size: 26 wide x 23 high

	Anchor	DMC
▫	1	blanc
	334	606
+	303	742
	238	703
	1031	3753
~	1010	951
	367	738
◇	368	437
■	403	310

French Knots: 403
Backstitch:
334 (2 strands)—reins
303 (2 strands)—mane
403—bear nose, horse eye & eyelashes
236/3799—remaining outlines

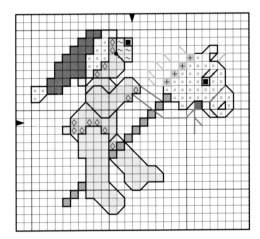

118

Design size: 25 wide x 35 high

	Anchor	DMC
▫	1	blanc
	73	963
⊙	75	962
	76	961
	1012	754
~	300	745
	311	3827
	1031	3753

	Kreinik
gold #4 braid	202HL

Eyelet (wand): gold #4 braid
Backstitch:
76—headband, gown, shoes
355/975—skin, wings, hair
gold #4 braid—halo, wand

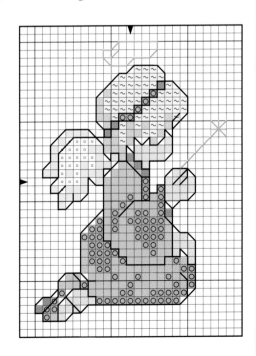

119

Design size: 29 wide x 17 high

	Anchor	DMC
■	334	606
⊙	314	741
~	302	743
	238	703
	97	554
	367	738
	398	415
■	403	310

French Knots: 403
Backstitch:
334 (2 strands)—mouse collar
351/400—bear
236/3799—mouse
403—train (except cowcatcher)
403 (2 strands)—cowcatcher

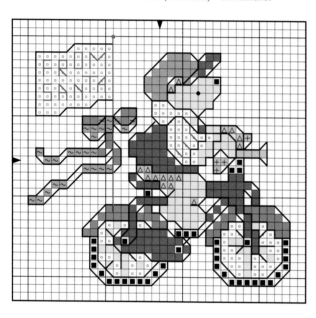

120

Design size: 34 wide x 31 high

	Anchor	DMC
▫	1	blanc
	334	606
	306	783
~	238	703
	227	701
	1031	3753
	130	809
	367	738
△	369	435
+	398	415
■	403	310

French Knots:
334 (2 strands)—flagpole
403—eye
Backstitch:
334—lettering, jacket stripes
334 (2 strands)—flagpole
403—bike, nose
236/3799—remaining outlines

121

Design size: 28 wide x 32 high

	Anchor	DMC
▫	1	blanc
	73	963
	46	666
	20	815
	314	741
	226	703
	1031	3753

Straight Stitch (scarf fringe): 401/413
French Knot: 149/311
Backstitch:
46—inside sign border
149—lettering
351/400—arms
401—remaining outlines

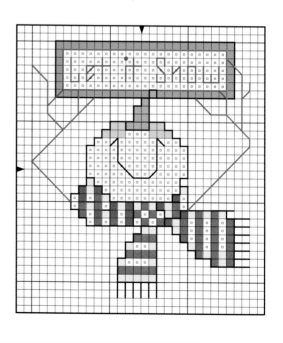

122

Design size: 25 wide x 30 high

	Anchor	DMC
▫	1	blanc
	334	606
~	46	666
	778	3774
△	8	3824
	131	798
	400	317

French Knots:
228/700—bow
236/3799—eyes, clothes

Backstitch:
46—candy cane, toy string
228—candy cane bow
236—remaining outlines

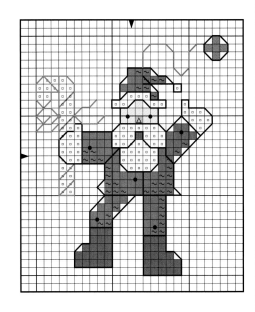

123

Design size: 36 wide x 35 high

	Anchor	DMC
▫	1	blanc
	885	739
	4146	950
~	868	353
∧	891	676
	1070	993
	1074	992
	1047	402
✕	1048	3776
	351	400
	393	640
■	403	310

Backstitch:
212/561—tree (except trunk)
340/920—nose, eyelids, mouth
905/3021—tree trunk
403—eyes, bell strap
236/3799—remaining outlines

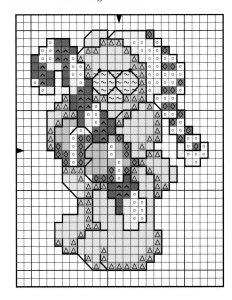

124

Design size: 23 wide x 30 high

	Anchor	DMC
▫	1	blanc
∧	334	606
	47	321
	238	703
◇	227	701
	1031	3753
~	1010	951
	367	738
△	369	435

French Knots: 403/310
Backstitch:
403—face
236/3799—remaining outlines

125

Design size: 28 wide x 30 high

	Anchor	DMC
	334	606
⊙	302	743
	225	702
	367	738
~	369	435
	832	612
■	403	310

French Knot: 403
Backstitch:
334—string
228/700—knob on string, tree (except trunk)
355/975—star
355 (2 strands)—tree trunk
403—nose, wheel
236/3799—remaining outlines

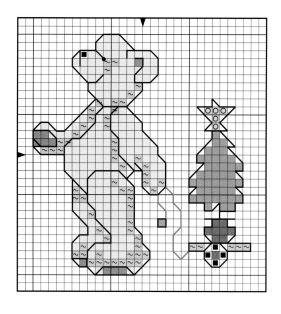

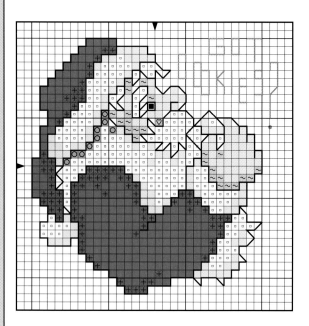

126

Design size: 32 wide x 32 high

	Anchor	DMC
▫	1	blanc
♡	36	3326
	334	606
+	47	321
	4146	950
~	868	353
	1031	3753
⊙	1033	932
■	403	310

French Knot: 131/798
Backstitch:
131—lettering
340/920—skin
403—eye
236/3799—remaining outlines

127

Design size: 23 wide x 30 high

	Anchor	DMC
▫	1	blanc
⊙	36	3326
	334	606
	47	321
	4146	950
	1031	3753
	369	435
	400	317
■	403	310

French Knots: 403
Backstitch:
403—boots, belt
236/3799—remaining outlines

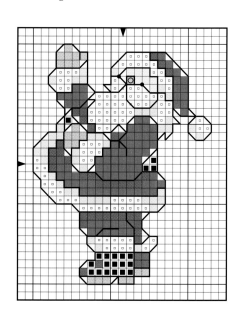

128

Design size: 11 wide x 13 high

Anchor	DMC	Backstitch:
1	blanc	302 (2 strands)—halo
778	3774	244/702—dress (except trim)
302	743	1049/3826—face, hands,
213	504	dress trim
261	989	358/801—hair, lyre
378	841	399/318—wings
234	762	

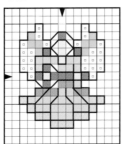

130

Design size: 12 wide x 13 high

Anchor	DMC	French Knot: 302 (2 strands)
1	blanc	**Backstitch:**
778	3774	302—wand
302	743	302 (2 strands)—halo
128	800	131/798—dress (except trim)
129	809	1049/3826—face, hand, dress trim
378	841	358/801—hair
234	762	399/318—wings

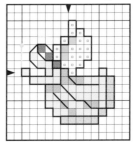

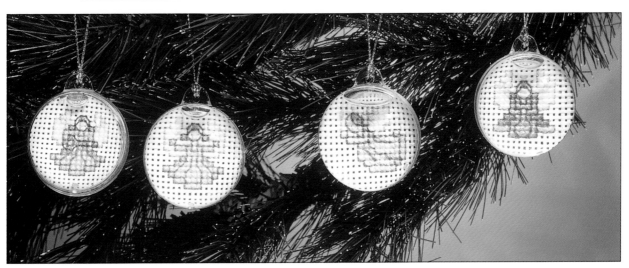

These angels stitch up in record time and therefore are ideal for ornaments and package ties.

129

Design size: 11 wide x 13 high

Anchor	DMC	Backstitch:
1	blanc	302 (2 strands)—halo
778	3774	1074/992—dress (except trim)
302	743	1049/3826—face, hands, dress trim
1092	959	358/801—hair
186	958	399/318—wings
378	841	
234	762	

131

Design size: 11 wide x 12 high

Anchor	DMC	Backstitch:
1	blanc	65/3685—dress (except trim)
66	3688	302 (2 strands)—halo
68	3687	1049/3826—face, hands,
778	3774	dress trim
302	743	358/801—hair
378	841	399/318—wings
234	762	

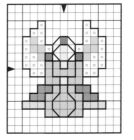

Santa and his toys bring joy to so many around the
world. With this bell pull and ornament, you can bring
some of that joy into your world.

132

Design size: 35 wide x 13 high

	Anchor	DMC
▫	1	blanc
▨	46	666
▨	226	703
☐	128	800
☒	130	809
▨	142	798

French Knot: 403/310

Backstitch:
22/814—berries
229/910—leaves
403—remaining outlines

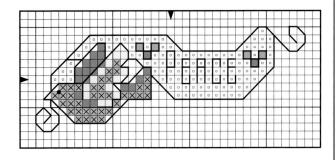

133

Design size: 29 wide x 37 high

	Anchor	DMC
▫	1	blanc
▨	334	606
∼	47	321
☐	778	3774
△	8	3824
☐	301	744
+	311	3827
▨	225	702
◉	227	701
☐	1031	3753
☐	130	809
∧	137	798
■	400	317

French Knots: 236/3799

Backstitch:
137—snow
236—remaining outlines

134

Design size: 35 wide x 32 high

	Anchor	DMC
▫	1	blanc
▨	334	606
▨	85	3609
☐	301	744
∼	311	3827
☐	225	702
▨	228	700

Backstitch:
110/208—sled tracery, green bag
tie & pattern
236/3799—remaining outlines

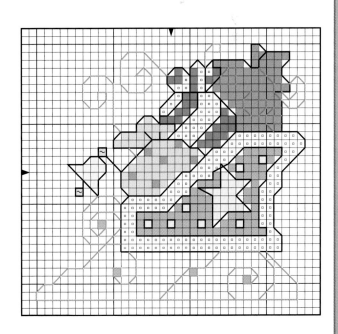

135

Design size: 31 wide x 29 high

	Anchor	DMC
□	1	blanc
■	46	666
□	301	744
▨	225	702
✕	228	700
▨	137	798
⌃	368	437
□	369	435

French Knots:
306/783—stars
236/3799—eye
Eyelets (small stars): 306
Backstitch:
306—large stars
137—rein
236—remaining outlines

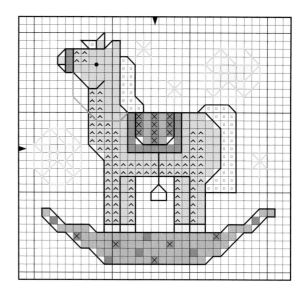

136

Design size: 28 wide x 30 high

	Anchor	DMC
□	1	blanc
▨	334	606
~	46	666
□	778	3774
□	301	744
□	891	676
⊙	306	783
□	225	702
▨	227	701
▨	131	798
▨	235	414
■	236	3799

French Knots: 236
Backstitch: 236

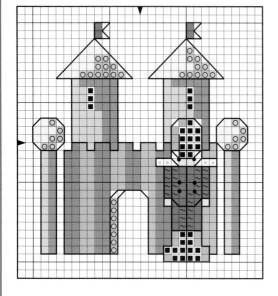

137

Design size: 30 wide x 33 high

	Anchor	DMC
□	1	blanc
△	1021	761
■	46	666
■	1006	304
+	215	320
▨	875	3813
□	1032	3752
▨	131	798
▨	110	208
~	1008	3773
□	234	762
■	400	317

Backstitch:
110—envelope lines
400—remaining outlines

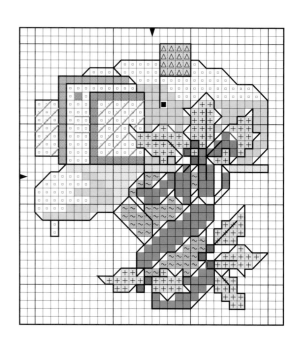

Santa is a wizard at creating joy and also checks his list to make sure all the world's children are on his flight plan.

138

Design size: 32 wide x 34 high

Anchor	DMC
1	blanc
895	223
334	606
4146	950
302	743
225	702
130	809
131	798

French Knots: 403/310
Eyelets: 306/783
Backstitch:
334 (2 strands)—wand, drumsticks, top
131—motion lines
236/3799—remaining outlines

139

Design size: 23 wide x 33 high

Anchor	DMC
1	blanc
334	606
47	321
4146	950
868	353
891	676
225	702
1031	3753
130	809
131	798
347	402
355	975
400	317
403	310

French Knots: 403
Backstitch:
403—boots
236/3799—remaining outlines

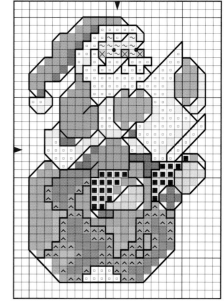

These sweet designs help us remember the important
parts of the holiday: peace, home, family, music, and love.

140

Design size: 16 wide x 29 high

Anchor	DMC
1	blanc
25	3326
1011	948
305	743
306	783
128	800
129	809
374	420

French Knots:
334/606—bow
1049/3826—ornament top

Backstitch:
334—bow
1049—hanger, ornament top & outline,
 horn, skin, bottom dress trim
131/798—remaining dress, wings
1050/3781—hair

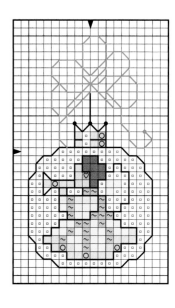

141

Design size: 16 wide x 29 high

Anchor	DMC
1	blanc
305	743
306	783
130	809
131	798
366	951
376	3774
378	841

French Knots:
334/606—berries
1049/3826—ornament top
131—bow
1086/839—eyes, nose

Backstitch:
1049—hanger, ornament top & outline
210/562—berry leaves
131—bow
132/797—clothes
1086—bear

142

Design size: 16 wide x 29 high

Anchor	DMC
1	blanc
334	606
47	321
305	743
306	783
206	564
209	913
211	562

French Knots:
1049/3826—ornament top
209—bow

Backstitch:
20/815—berries
1049—hanger, ornament top & outline
209—bow
211—leaves

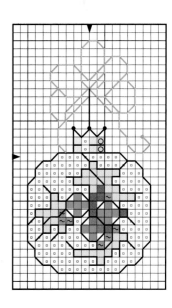

143

Design size: 25 wide x 30 high

Anchor	DMC
1	blanc
334	606
1012	754
301	744
890	729
225	702
1031	3573

Kreinik
gold #4 braid 202HL
French Knots: 236/3799
Backstitch:
334—dress trim
227/701—dress trim, harp strings
131/798—wings
gold #4 braid—halo
236—remaining outlines

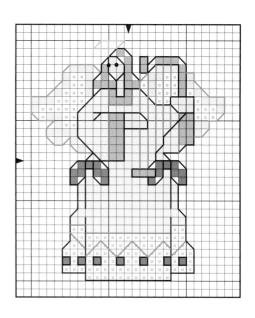

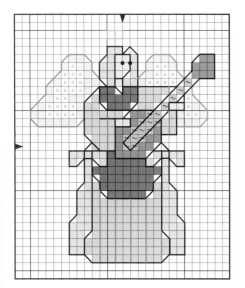

144

Design size: 24 wide x 29 high

Anchor	DMC
1	blanc
334	606
1012	754
305	743
209	913
1031	3753
376	3774
379	840

Kreinik
gold #4 braid 202HL
French Knots: 236/3799
Backstitch:
gold #4 braid—halo
210/562—dress trim
131/798—wings
236—remaining outlines

145

Design size: 23 wide x 23 high

Anchor	DMC
1	blanc
1012	754
891	676
306	783
131	798
1047	402
376	3774
379	840

Kreinik
gold #4 braid 202HL
French Knots: 891
Eyelet (star): gold #4 braid
Backstitch:
308/781—border, head, hay
936/632—remaining outlines

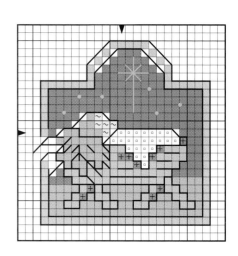

146

Design size: 27 wide x 21 high

	Anchor	DMC
□	1	blanc
▓	46	666
▒	225	702

French Knots:
47/321—berries
403/310—eye
Backstitch:
46—lettering
229/910—leaves
131/798—dove (except beak & legs)
355/975—beak, legs

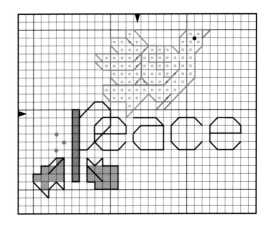

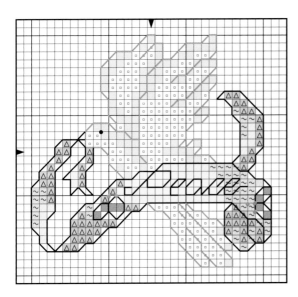

147

Design size: 31 wide x 29 high

	Anchor	DMC
□	1	blanc
□	301	744
~	311	3827
△	306	783
▓	225	702
□	1031	3753

French Knots:
334/606—berries
236/3799—eye
Backstitch:
227/701—lettering
131/798—dove (except beak)
355/975—banner
236—beak, leaves

148

Design size: 25 wide x 28 high

	Anchor	DMC
□	1	blanc
▲	46	666
▓	47	321
□	301	744
~	302	743
▒	227	701
+	129	809
▒	109	209
□	366	951
▓	378	841
▒	234	762

French Knot: 403/310
Backstitch:
46—basket stripes
229/910—branches
400/317—remaining outlines

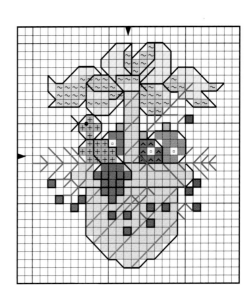

What is Christmas without handmade stockings hanging from
the mantel and shiny glass ornaments hanging on the tree?

149

Design size: 24 wide x 30 high

	Anchor	DMC
□	1	blanc
	49	3689
∿	40	956
∧	46	666
	20	815
	316	970
	305	743
△	303	742
	240	966
◇	226	703
	229	910
	128	800
♡	130	809
	142	798

Backstitch:
20—berries
229—leaves
132/797—ornament
403/310—string

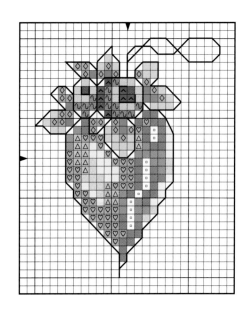

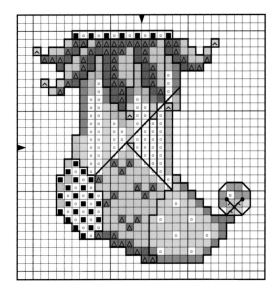

150

Design size: 28 wide x 29 high

	Anchor	DMC
□	1	blanc
	40	956
△	46	666
	20	815
	316	970
	305	743
∧	303	742
	226	703
	229	910
	231	453
■	403	310

French Knots: 403
Backstitch:
20—top stocking stripes
403—remaining outlines

151

Design size: 23 wide x 30 high

	Anchor	DMC
□	1	blanc
	40	956
~	334	606
△	46	666
	20	815
	306	783
	1048	3776
	240	966
⊠	226	703
	229	910
	231	453

Backstitch:
229—heart stripes
340/920—loops
403/310—remaining outlines

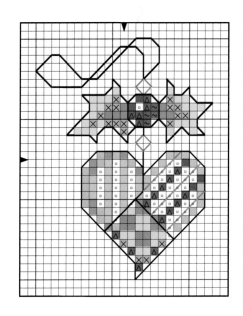

152

Design size: 28 wide x 34 high

Anchor	DMC
1	blanc
46	666
20	815
316	970
305	743
303	742
128	800

French Knots: 403/310
Backstitch:
46—cuff chevrons
20—remaining stocking
316—bell outlines
403—bell slits, string

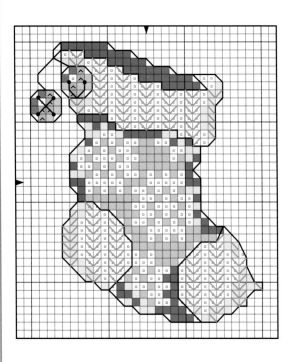

154

Design size: 32 wide x 35 high

Anchor	DMC
1	blanc
46	666
20	815
316	970
305	743
303	742
240	966
226	703
142	798
139	797

French Knots: 403/310
Backstitch:
46—heel & toe grid
316—bell outlines
142—cuff chevrons
139—remaining stocking
403—bell slits, string

153

Design size: 30 wide x 35 high

Anchor	DMC
1	blanc
316	970
305	743
303	742
226	703
229	910
128	800

French Knots: 403/310
Backstitch:
316—bell outlines
226—cuff, heel, & toe chevrons
229—remaining stocking
403—bell slits, string

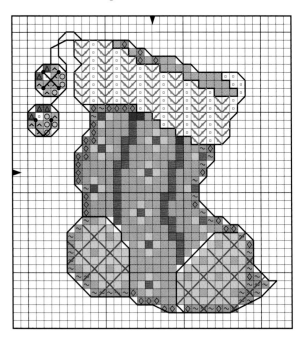

155

Design size: 11 wide x 26 high

	Anchor	DMC
	40	956
△	46	666
	20	815
+	316	970
	1048	3776
~	305	743
∧	303	742
	240	966
✕	226	703
	229	910

Backstitch:
20—red ornament tip
229—remaining ornament (except top), string
340/920—ornament top

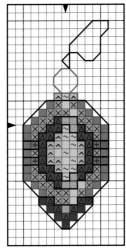

156

Design size: 18 wide x 23 high

	Anchor	DMC
○	334	606
△	46	666
	20	815
+	316	970
	326	720
~	305	743
∧	303	742
	240	966
✕	226	703
	229	910

Backstitch:
20—red ornament edges, center motifs, string
229—green ornament borders
340/920—ornament top

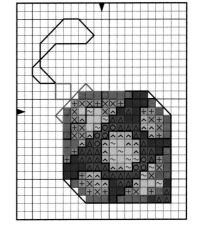

157

Design size: 19 wide x 28 high

	Anchor	DMC
▫	1	blanc
	305	743
~	303	742
	128	800
	130	809
✕	142	798
■	139	797
	109	209

Backstitch:
139—ornament (except top), string
340/920—top

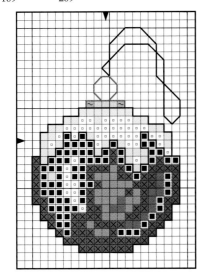

158

Design size: 30 wide x 24 high

	Anchor	DMC
▫	1	blanc
	48	3689
+	85	3609
~	87	3607
	94	917
	303	742

Backstitch:
101/550—ornament (except top), string
340/920—top

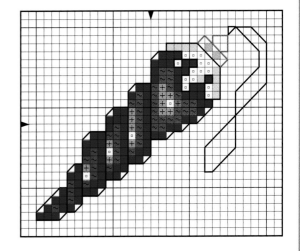

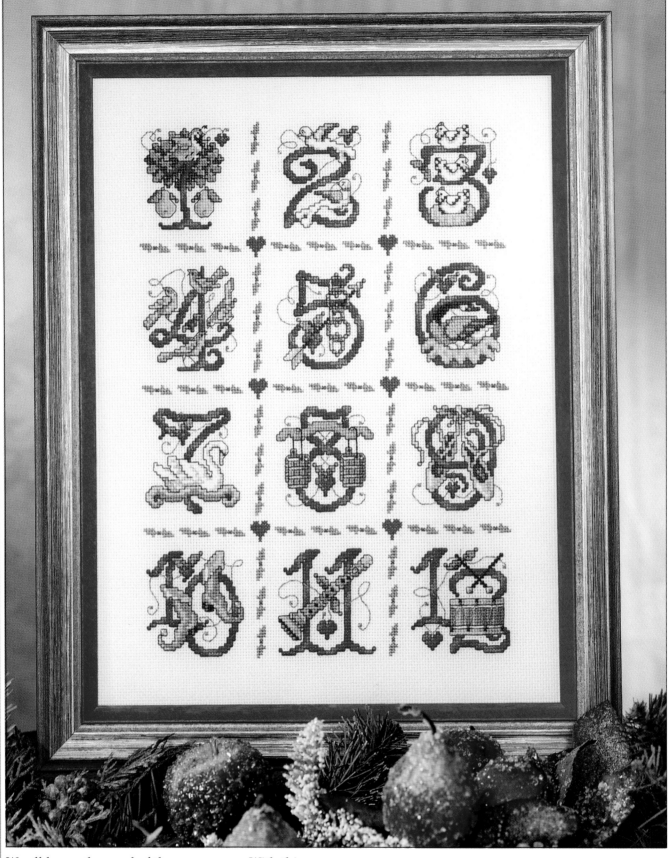

We all know the carol of the same name. With this
elegant sampler we will never forget this classic carol so
happily in tune with Christmas giving.

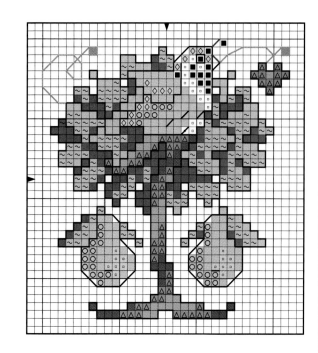

159

Design size: 32 wide x 35 high

Anchor	DMC	Kreinik
1	blanc	
11	351	gold #4 braid 202HL
13	347	**Backstitch:**
43	814	1 (2 strands)—around eye
313	742	382 (2 strands)—head tuft,
891	676	chest markings
363	436	gold #4 braid—tendrils
369	435	360/898—remaining outlines
265	3347	
243	703	
212	561	
382	3371	
398	415	

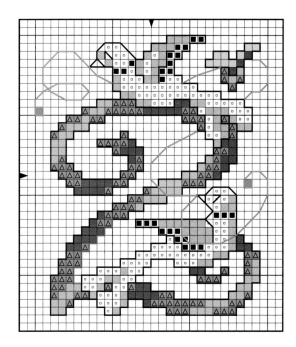

160

Design size: 30 wide x 35 high

Anchor	DMC	Kreinik
1	blanc	gold #4 braid 202HL
11	351	**Backstitch:**
13	347	400 (2 strands)—eyes
43	814	gold #4 braid—tendrils
243	703	360/898—remaining outlines
212	561	
398	415	
400	317	

161

Design size: 31 wide x 35 high

Anchor	DMC	Kreinik
1	blanc	gold #4 braid 202HL
11	351	**French Knots:** 382
13	347	**Backstitch:**
43	814	gold #4 braid—tendrils
891	676	360/898—remaining outlines
363	436	
243	703	
212	561	
382	3371	
398	415	

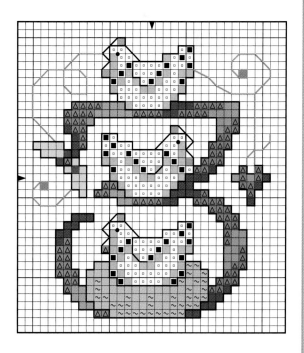

162

Design size: 34 wide x 35 high

Anchor	DMC
11	351
13	347
43	814
891	676
~ 363	436
243	703
212	561
⊙ 167	519
161	813

		Kreinik
	gold #4 braid	202HL

French Knots: 382/3371
Backstitch:
gold #4 braid—tendrils
360/898—remaining outlines

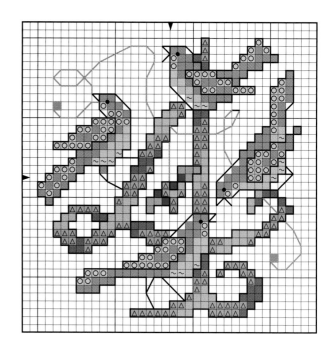

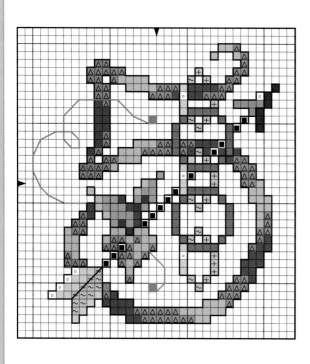

163

Design size: 32 wide x 35 high

Anchor	DMC
▫ 1	blanc
11	351
△ 13	347
43	814
891	676
~ 363	436
+ 369	435
265	3347
243	703
212	561
■ 382	3371
399	318
400	317

		Kreinik
	gold #4 braid	202HL

Backstitch:
gold #4 braid—tendril
360/898—remaining outlines

164

Design size: 30 wide x 35 high

Anchor	DMC
▫ 1	blanc
11	351
△ 13	347
43	814
891	676
⊙ 363	436
243	703
212	561
1082	841
✕ 1084	840
360	898
■ 382	3371
398	415
400	317

		Kreinik
	gold #4 braid	202HL

Backstitch:
gold #4 braid—tendrils
360—remaining outlines

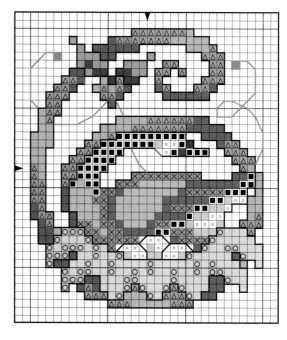

165

Design size: 34 wide x 35 high

	Anchor	DMC			Kreinik
□	1	blanc	■	gold #4 braid	202HL
	11	351		**Backstitch:**	
△	13	347		gold #4 braid—tendrils	
	43	814		360—remaining outlines	
	313	742			
	243	703			
	212	561			
	167	519			
	161	813			
◎	360	898			
■	382	3371			
	231	453			
~	399	318			

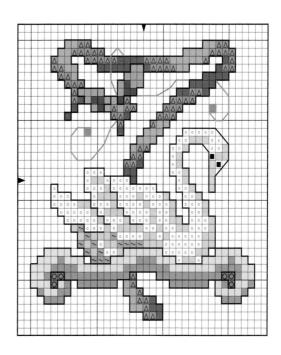

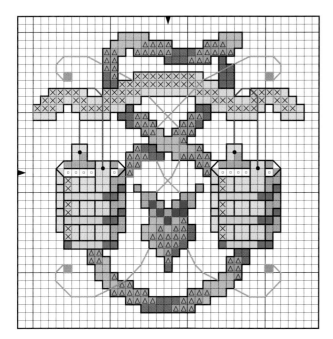

166

Design size: 35 wide x 35 high

	Anchor	DMC			Kreinik
□	1	blanc	■	gold #4 braid	202HL
	11	351		**French Knots:** 382/3371	
△	13	347		**Backstitch:**	
	43	814		382 (2 strands)—pail handles	
×	363	436		gold #4 braid—tendrils	
	243	703		360/898—remaining outlines	
	212	561			
	369	435			
	370	434			
	398	415			
	235	414			

167

Design size: 33 wide x 35 high

	Anchor	DMC
□	1	blanc
	11	351
△	13	347
	43	814
	891	676
~	363	436
	265	3347
+	243	703
	212	561
◎	1084	840
^	360	898

		Kreinik
	gold #4 braid	202HL

Backstitch:
gold #4 braid—tendrils
360—remaining outlines

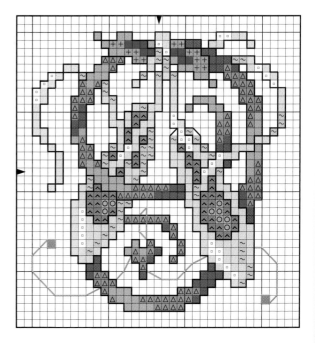

168

Design size: 35 wide x 35 high

Anchor	DMC
1	blanc
11	351
13	347
43	814
891	676
363	436
243	703
212	561
167	519
161	813
382	3371
400	317

	Kreinik
gold #4 braid	202HL

Backstitch:
gold #4 braid—tendrils
360/898—remaining outlines

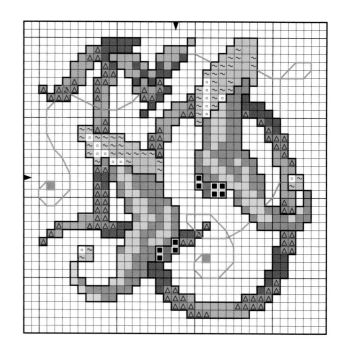

169

Design size: 35 wide x 35 high

Anchor	DMC
11	351
13	347
43	814
891	676
363	436
265	3347
243	703
212	561
1082	841
1084	840
382	3371

	Kreinik
gold #4 braid	202HL

Backstitch:
gold #4 braid—tendrils
360/898—remaining outlines

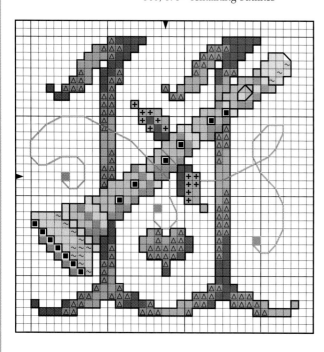

170

Design size: 35 wide x 35 high

Anchor	DMC
1	blanc
11	351
13	347
43	814
891	676
363	436
243	703
212	561
167	519
161	813
162	517
382	3371
398	415
400	317

	Kreinik
gold #4 braid	202HL

Straight Stitch (tuning strings): gold #4 braid
Backstitch:
gold #4 braid—tendrils
360/898—remaining outlines

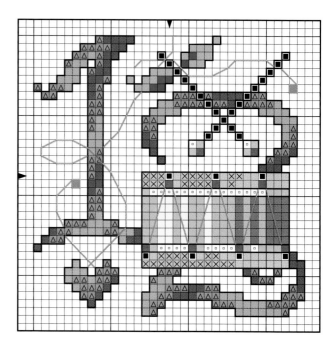

Don't forget to leave Santa a special Christmas Eve treat!

171

Design size: 29 wide x 33 high

	Anchor	DMC
▫	1	blanc
♡	36	3326
	334	606
	4146	950
~	868	353
	228	700
	1031	3753
△	129	809
	131	798

Backstitch:
131—eyes
340/920—skin
403/310—glasses
236/3799—remaining outlines

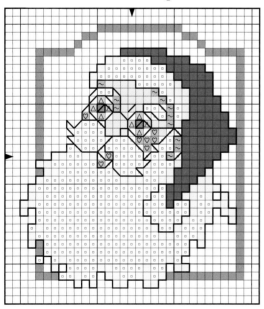

172

Design size: 30 wide x 31 high

	Anchor	DMC
▫	1	blanc
○	36	3326
	895	223
	334	606
	4146	950
~	868	353
	1031	3753
	921	931
■	403	310

Backstitch:
340/920—skin
403—eyes
236/3799—remaining outlines

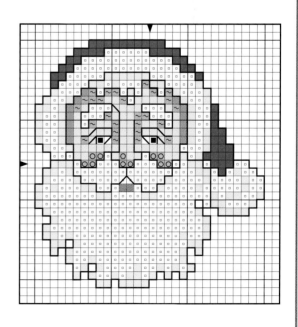

Santa and his friends engage in activities they most
enjoy, including a nap!

173

Design size: 34 wide x 35 high

Anchor	DMC
1	blanc
49	3689
40	956
46	666
22	814
316	970
326	720
240	966
226	703
229	910
231	453

Backstitch:
40—cheek
229—heart stripes
403/310—remaining outlines

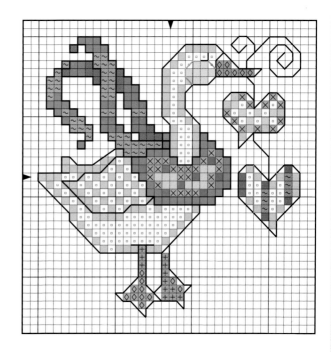

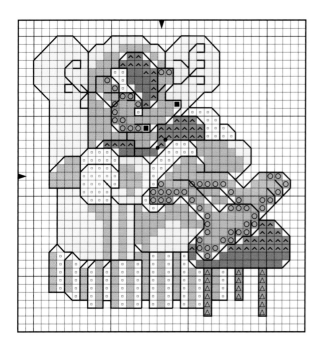

174

Design size: 33 wide x 35 high

Anchor	DMC	
1	blanc	
334	606	
47	321	
225	702	
128	800	
130	809	
1048	3776	
1008	3773	
1007	3772	
403	310	

French Knots: 403
Backstitch: 403

175

Design size: 31 wide x 35 high

Anchor	DMC
1	blanc
334	606
47	321
4146	950
868	353
241	966
226	703
1032	3752
368	437
369	435
398	415
235	414
403	310

Backstitch:
340/920—skin
403—eyes
236/3799—remaining outlines

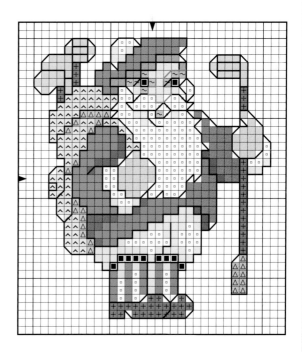

176

Design size: 24 wide x 19 high

Anchor	DMC
1	blanc
8	3824
301	744
240	966
129	809

French Knots: 403/310
Backstitch:
131/798—motion lines
355/975—beak, feet, leg
236/3799—remaining outlines

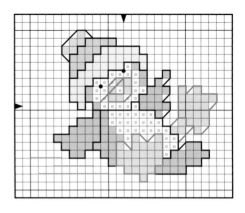

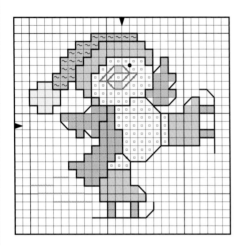

177

Design size: 24 wide x 23 high

Anchor	DMC
1	blanc
49	3689
8	3824
301	744
240	966
129	809

French Knot: 403/310
Backstitch:
131/798—motion lines
355/975—beak
236/3799—remaining outlines

178

Design size: 23 wide x 29 high

Anchor	DMC
40	956
46	666
374	420
226	703
229	910
130	809
137	798
90	554
98	553
1047	402
1048	3776
403	310

Backstitch:
403—eyes
401/413—remaining outlines

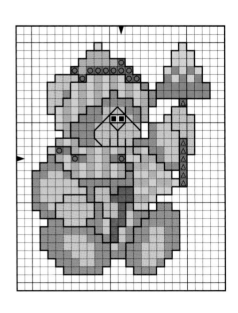

179

Design size: 24 wide x 25 high

	Anchor	DMC
▫	1	blanc
▓	334	606
☐	1031	3753
☐	368	437
~	369	435
■	403	310

Backstitch:
403—eyes, nose
236/3799—remaining outlines

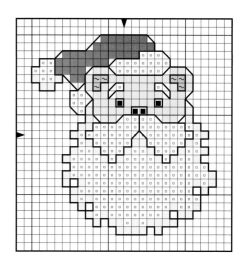

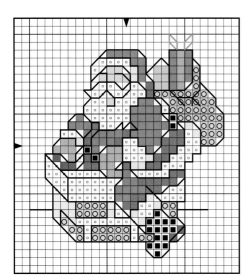

180

Design size: 25 wide x 28 high

	Anchor	DMC
▫	1	blanc
▓	334	606
▓	47	321
☐	4146	950
☐	238	703
☐	1031	3753
☐	95	554
◎	347	402
▓	400	317
■	403	310

Backstitch:
227/701—package bow
403—eyes, belt, boots
236/3799—remaining outlines

181

Design size: 24 wide x 29 high

	Anchor	DMC
▫	1	blanc
~	894	223
+	1027	3722
☐	4146	950
♡	868	353
▷	361	738
◎	362	437
☐	1070	993
◇	1074	992
▓	1082	841
■	403	310

French Knot: 403

Backstitch:
340/920—Santa's nose, rabbit
403—Santa's eyes
236/3799—remaining outlines

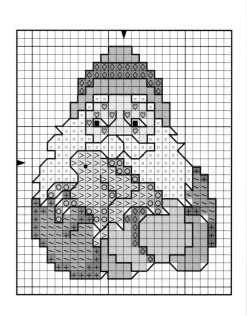

Festive designs will enhance your table at special
holiday gatherings of friends and family.

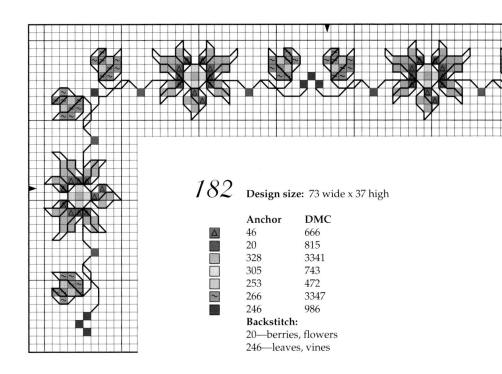

182

Design size: 73 wide x 37 high

Anchor	DMC
46	666
20	815
328	3341
305	743
253	472
266	3347
246	986

Backstitch:
20—berries, flowers
246—leaves, vines

183

Design size: 19 wide x 11 high

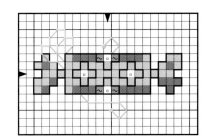

Anchor	DMC
1	blanc
302	743
1002	977
129	809
131	798

French Knots: 302
Backstitch:
302—strings
139/797—cracker

184

Design size: 77 wide x 36 high

Anchor	DMC	Backstitch:
1020	3713	897/221—pomegranates
1022	760	217—leaves, stems
1027	3722	136—blue dots
336	758	349—flowers
1043	369	
261	989	
217	561	
136	799	
349	301	

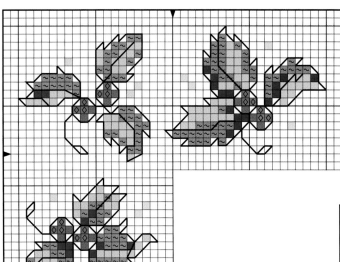

185

Design size: 40 wide x 32 high

	Anchor	DMC
◇	334	606
	47	321
	302	743
	253	472
~	266	3347
	246	986

Backstitch:
20/815—berries
246—leaves
374/420—stems

186

Design size: 35 wide x 34 high
Note: use alphabet below

	Anchor	DMC
	46	666
	242	989
	210	562

French Knots:
46—colon for "To"
212/561—colon for "From"

Backstitch:
46—berries, "To," border
210—leaves, "From," names

187

Design size: 32 wide x 29 high
Note: use alphabet below

	Anchor	DMC
	46	666
	300	745
	311	3827
	208	563
	210	562

French Knots: 46
Backstitch:
46—berries, lettering, names
308/781—bow
212/561—leaves

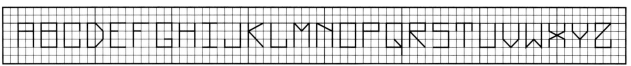

Quick-to-stitch designs personalize your gift tags on 14-count perforated plastic.

188

Design size: 33 wide x 16 high

	Anchor	DMC
□	1	blanc
~	302	743
▨	131	798
▢	368	437

French Knots:
46/666—berries
20/815—lettering
Backstitch:
20—lettering
229/910—branches
400/317—remaining outlines

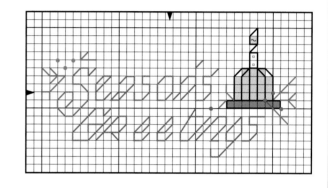

189

Design size: 28 wide x 12 high
Note: use alphabet on page 82

	Anchor	DMC
~	334	606
▨	46	666
▢	302	743

French Knots: 210/562
Backstitch:
210—lettering, names
236/3799—flower

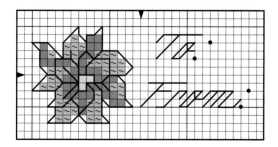

190

Design size: 37 wide x 14 high

	Anchor	DMC
~	334	606
▨	46	666
▢	302	743

Backstitch:
210/562—lettering
236/3799—flower

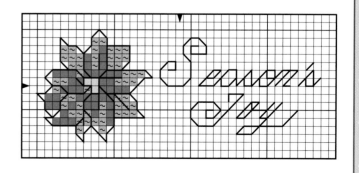

Holiday sweets beautifully stitched into a red and
green bordered sampler will last generations—unlike
the home-baked variety.

191

Design size: 29 wide x 33 high

	Anchor	DMC
▫	1	blanc
	73	963
~	40	956
	29	309
+	334	606
△	46	666
	20	815
	240	966
○	226	703
	229	910
	1031	3753
	1048	3776
	357	433

Backstitch:
1 (2 strands)—cupcake
  cherry highlight
20—cherries, pink frosting
229—leaves
137/798—white frosting
357—cake, cupcake, stems

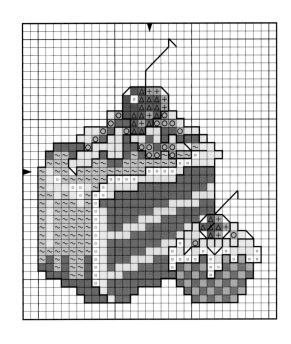

192

Design size: 28 wide x 29 high

	Anchor	DMC		Anchor	DMC
▫	1	blanc		229	910
	49	3689		167	519
	40	956	○	168	3810
	334	606		169	806
✕	46	666	◇	340	920
	20	815			
	316	970			
	305	743			
~	303	742			
	240	966			
△	226	703			

Backstitch:
20—berries, stripe, clapper
229—leaves
169—ribbon
340—remaining bell

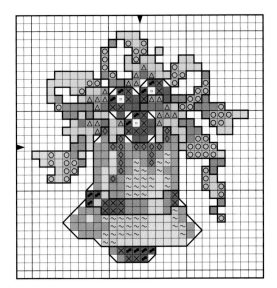

193

Design size: 26 wide x 30 high

	Anchor	DMC
▫	1	blanc
	50	605
	40	956
○	334	606
⁄	46	666
	20	815
~	305	743
◇	303	742
	240	966
✕	226	703
	229	910
	99	552
	1047	402
	1048	3776

Backstitch:
20—cherries, frosting
229—leaves
381/938—stems, cupcake paper

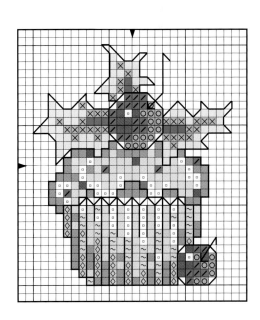

194

Design size: 28 wide x 30 high

Anchor	DMC
1	blanc
40	956
334	606
46	666
20	815
305	743
303	742
316	970
326	720
253	472

Anchor	DMC
240	966
226	703
229	910
1031	3753
1048	3776

Backstitch:
20—lollipop, berries
229—leaves
371/434—bow, stick

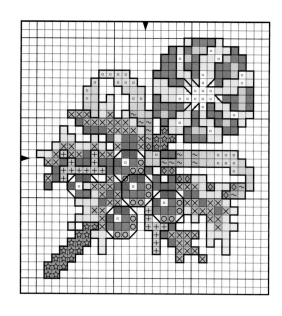

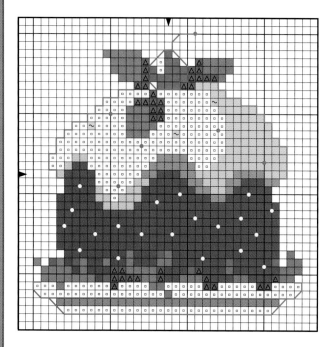

195

Design size: 35 wide x 35 high

Anchor	DMC
1	blanc
46	666
1094	604
86	3608
240	966
256	704
268	469
136	799
352	300

French Knots:
1 (2 strands)—pudding
46—sauce, stem
Backstitch: 46

196

Design size: 27 wide x 34 high

Anchor	DMC
1	blanc
334	606
9046	321
1094	604
86	3608
313	742
293	727
254	3348
242	989

Backstitch:
324/721—yellow cane outline
9046—remaining outlines

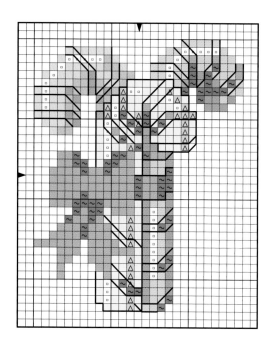

197

Design size: 34 wide x 18 high

	Anchor	DMC
▫	1	blanc
■	46	666
~	311	3827
■	1047	402
□	240	966
⊙	226	703
■	229	910
△	357	433
■	381	938

Backstitch:
20/815—berries
229—leaves
381—cookies

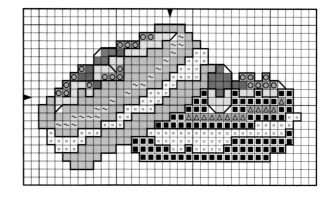

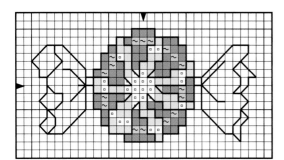

198

Design size: 29 wide x 14 high

	Anchor	DMC
▫	1	blanc
~	240	966
■	226	703
□	1031	3753

Backstitch:
229/910—inner candy lines
403/310—remaining outlines

199

Design size: 31 wide x 25 high

	Anchor	DMC
▫	1	blanc
~	334	606
■	46	666
■	20	815
□	300	745
□	240	966
■	226	703
□	1031	3753
■	1047	402
△	1048	3776
■	357	433
■	381	938

Backstitch:
20—cherry
229/910—green candy
137/798—green candy frosting
381—remaining outlines

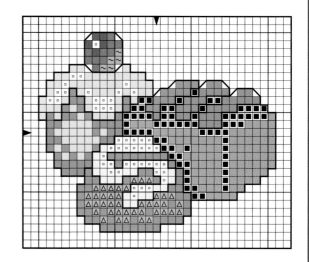

200

Design size: 35 wide x 34 high

	Anchor	DMC
□	1	blanc
	1094	604
	46	666
	1005	816
	292	3078
~	302	743
	228	700
	108	210

French Knots: 334/606
Backstitch:
334—string, inner round peppermint
  stripes, other peppermint, cranberry
235/414—round peppermint outline
  & wrapper, popcorn

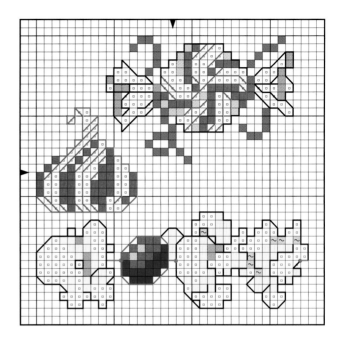

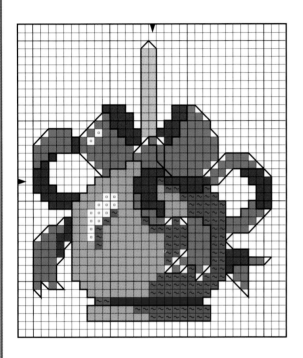

201

Design size: 31 wide x 35 high

	Anchor	DMC
□	1	blanc
	334	606
~	9046	321
	1005	816
	362	437
	228	700
	941	792

Backstitch:
1005—apple
941—ribbon, stick

202

Design size: 34 wide x 30 high

	Anchor	DMC		Anchor	DMC
□	1	blanc		229	910
	40	956		128	800
	46	666		130	809
	20	815		90	554
	305	743	△	97	553
~	303	742		99	552
◇	316	970	**Backstitch:**		
	240	966	99—ribbon candy line		
○	226	703	403/310—remaining outlines		

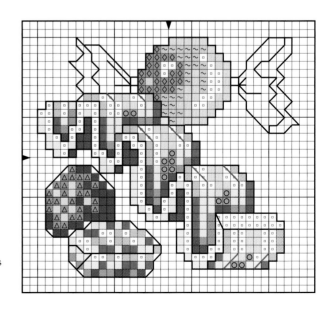

Two cute bears adorn greeting cards made from perforated paper.

203

Design size: 18 wide x 35 high

Anchor	DMC	French Knots: 403
1	blanc	**Backstitch:**
334	606	334—sleeve & hem stripes
47	321	47—roses, hollyberries
300	745	229/910—leaves
302	743	131/798—wings, candles
238	703	355/975—bear (except nose),
227	701	candle flames & wicks
1031	3753	236/3799—dress, shoes
367	738	403—nose
403	310	

204

Design size: 31 wide x 28 high

Anchor	DMC	French Knots: 403
885	739	**Backstitch:**
334	606	403—nose, birds
130	809	905/3021 (2 strands)—cross
131	798	905—remaining outlines
367	738	
369	435	
1048	3776	
1049	3826	
392	642	
393	3790	
904	640	
403	310	

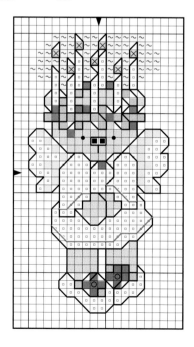

The nativity, one reason we celebrate Christmas, is depicted
on a simple yet elegant sampler. An angel ornament and
bookmarks add a religious perspective to the season.

205

Design size: 32 wide x 33 high

Anchor	DMC
11	351
13	347
301	744
204	563
1074	992
160	827
108	210
110	208
362	437
369	435
371	434
378	841
1088	838

	Kreinik
gold #4 braid	202HL

Backstitch:
gold #4 braid—crown
1088 (2 strands)—camel's eye
1088—remaining outlines

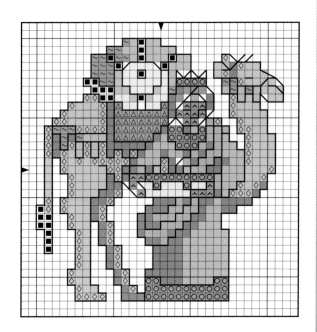

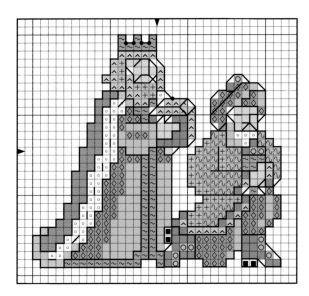

206

Design size: 32 wide x 29 high

Anchor	DMC		Anchor	DMC
1	blanc		1088	838
6	754		398	415
11	351			
13	347			**Kreinik**
891	676		gold #4 braid	202HL
363	436			
204	563			
1074	992			
110	208			
369	435			
371	434			

French Knots:
11 (2 strands)—crown
11 (3 strands)—box
Backstitch:
1088 (2 strands)—mustaches
1088—remaining outlines

207

Design size: 35 wide x 35 high

Anchor	DMC
1	blanc
6	754
891	676
363	436
301	744
204	563
1074	992
160	827
161	813
108	210
110	208
369	435
378	841
1084/1086	840/839
1088	838
398	415

	Kreinik
gold # 4 braid	202HL

French Knots: 1088
Straight Stitch (star):
gold #4 braid
Backstitch:
1084/1086 (1 strand of each)—mustache
1088 (2 strands)—Mary's bangs
1088—remaining outlines

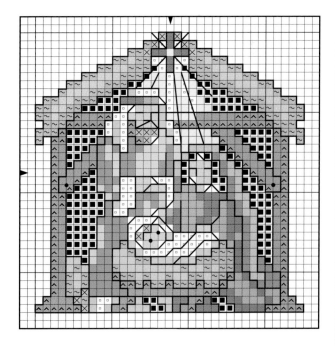

208

Design size: 26 wide x 31 high

Anchor	DMC
1	blanc
6	754
891	676
363	436
204	563
1074	992
160	827
161	813
369	435
371	434
378	841
382	3371
398	415
400	317

Backstitch:
1088/838 (2 strands)—mustache
1088—remaining outlines

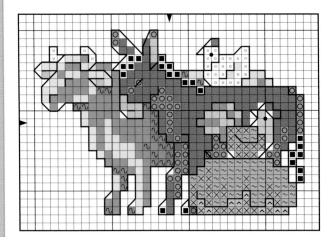

209

Design size: 35 wide x 23 high

Anchor	DMC
1	blanc
13	347
4146	950
891	676
363	436
369	435
204	563
1074	992
378	841
1084/1086	840/839
1088	838
398	415
235	414
400	317

French Knots: 1088
Backstitch:
891 (2 strands)—beaks
1088 (2 strands)—eyes, nostrils
1088—remaining outlines

210

Design size: 35 wide x 30 high

Anchor	DMC
6	754
386	3823
301	744
363	436
1060	3811
160	827
161	813
869	3743

	Kreinik
gold #4 braid	202HL

Backstitch:
gold #4 braid—halo
1088/838 (2 strands)—lettering
1088—remaining outlines

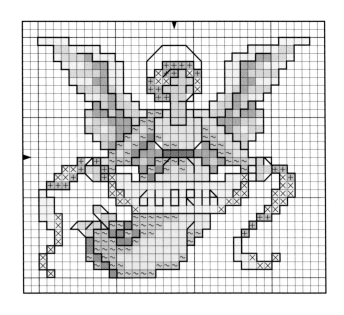

211

Design size: 22 wide x 22 high

	Anchor	DMC
□	1	blanc
~	96	3609
	778	3774
	301	744
◎	306	783
	253	472
	128	800
■	355	975

Kreinik
gold #4 braid   202HL
French Knot: gold #4 braid
Eyelet (star): gold #4 braid
Backstitch:
306—halo
227/701—tree
131/798—wings
355—hair, skin, tree stump, ornaments
400/317—robe, shoes

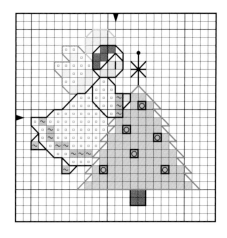

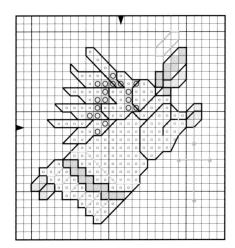

212

Design size: 23 wide x 24 high

	Anchor	DMC
□	1	blanc
◎	386	3823
	778	3774
	302	743

Kreinik
gold #4 braid   202HL
French Knots: gold #4 braid
Backstitch:
302—robe stripes
gold #4 braid—cross, halo
355/975—remaining outlines

213

Design size: 22 wide x 24 high

	Anchor	DMC
□	1	blanc
	96	3609
	778	3774
	301	744
~	302	743
	185	964
+	109	209
	1047	402
△	1048	3776

Kreinik
gold #4 braid   202HL
Eyelet (star): gold #4 braid
Backstitch:
302—halo
131/798—swaddling, clothes
1048—roof, skin

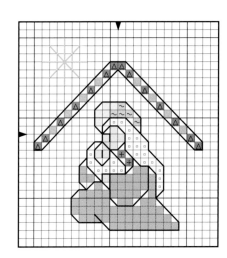

Sweet and beautiful angels and happy snowmen
are bound to bring good cheer to any home.

214

Design size: 27 wide x 29 high

Anchor	DMC
1	blanc
333	608
778	3774
314	741
306	783
386	3823
301	744
1048	3776

Kreinik	
gold #4 braid	202HL

French Knots: 403/310
Backstitch:
76/961—mouth
333—robe stripes (except sleeves)
306—wings, light glow
226/703—sleeve stripes
131/798—candle
355/975—hair, skin, candle holder, flame
gold #4 braid—halo
400/317—remaining outlines

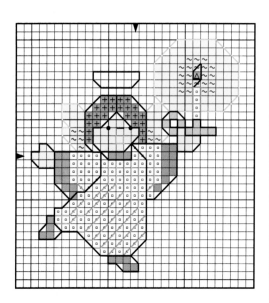

215

Design size: 28 wide x 30 high

Anchor	DMC
301	744
302	743
1002	977
129	800
131	798

Backstitch:
1002—light rays
130/809—portion of "Y" in the light
131—remaining lettering
1049/3826—cross

216

Design size: 30 wide x 22 high

Anchor	DMC
1	blanc
46	666
96	3609
778	3774
302	743
225	702
1092	959
186	958
128	800
109	209
1047	402

Backstitch:
228/700—wreath
187/3812—sleeve stripes
131/798—wing
355/975—hair, halo, skin
400/317—remaining outlines

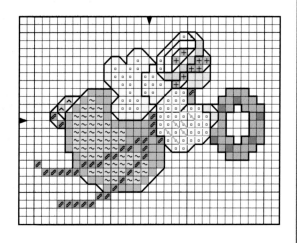

217

Design size: 25 wide x 27 high

	Anchor	DMC
▫	1	blanc
▨	302	743
◻	128	800
▨	342	211

Backstitch:
355/975—stars, windows
131/798—remaining outlines

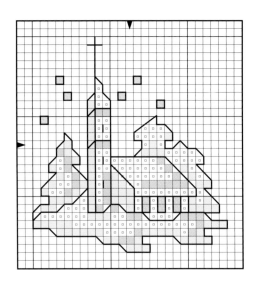

218

Design size: 27 wide x 26 high

	Anchor	DMC
▫	1	blanc
▨	46	666
◻	778	3774
◻	301	744
▨	228	700
◻	128	800
~	342	211
▨	109	209
+	1048	3776

French Knot: 403/310

Backstitch:
306/783—halo, ornaments
228—tree
131/798—wings, dove
355/975—hair, skin
400/317—remaining outlines

219

Design size: 18 wide x 19 high

	Anchor	DMC
▫	1	blanc
~	73	963
♡	75	962
◻	778	3774
◻	300	745

	Kreinik
gold #4 braid	202HL

Backstitch:
76/961—robe trim
131/798—wings
355/975—hair, skin
gold #4 braid—halo
400/317—remaining outlines

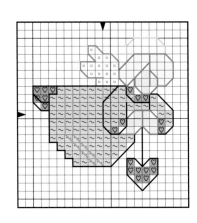

220

Design size: 30 wide x 30 high

Anchor	DMC
1	blanc
778	3774
225	702
228	700
128	800
103	211
108	210
110	208
1047	402

	Kreinik
gold #4 braid	202HL

Backstitch:
228—bodice stripes
131/798—wings
1049/3826—hair, skin (except eyes),
   hands, feet
400/317—dress, shoes
403/310—eyes
gold #4 braid—halo

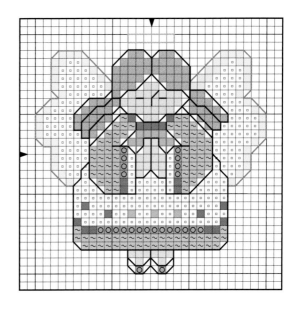

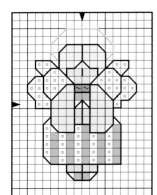

221

Design size: 14 wide x 19 high

Anchor	DMC
1	blanc
778	3774
301	744
185	964
128	800
130	809

	Kreinik
gold #4 braid	202HL

Backstitch:
131/798—wings, dress, shoes
355/975—hair, skin
gold #4 braid—halo

222

Design size: 33 wide x 17 high

Anchor	DMC
1	blanc
778	3774
386	3823
311	3827
86	3608
128	800
1047	402

	Kreinik
gold #4 braid	202HL

Backstitch:
131/798—wings
355/975—hair, banner, skin
400/317—robes
gold #4 braid—halos

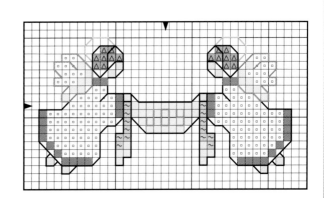

223

Design size: 23 wide x 30 high

	Anchor	DMC
▫	1	blanc
	73	963
△	75	962
	306	783
	128	800
	366	951
~	1047	402
■	403	310
	Kreinik	
	gold #4 braid	202HL

French Knots: 403
Backstitch:
76/961—sleeve & hem stripes
306—harp strings
131/798—wings
1049/3826—bear (except nose),
    remaining harp
400/317—gown, shoes
403—nose
gold #4 braid—halo

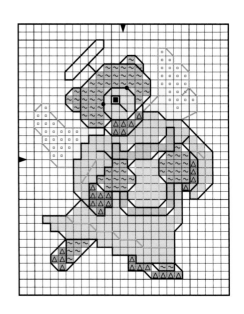

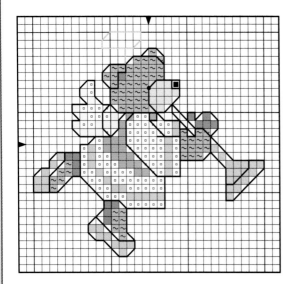

224

Design size: 30 wide x 28 high

	Anchor	DMC
▫	1	blanc
	313	742
	185	964
	128	800
	108	210
	366	951
~	1047	402
	1048	3776
■	403	310

	Kreinik
gold #4 braid	202HL

French Knot: 403
Backstitch:
131/798—wings, gown, shoes
403—nose
gold #4 braid—halo
1049/3826—remaining outlines

225

Design size: 27 wide x 29 high

	Anchor	DMC
▫	1	blanc
O	885	739
∧	306	783
	301	744
☆	302	743
	238	703
	1031	3753
~	367	738
✕	369	435
	355	975
■	403	310

French Knot: 403
Backstitch:
306—halo, star
131/798—bird
229/910—tree (except trunk)
355—bear (except nose),
    tree trunk
403—nose

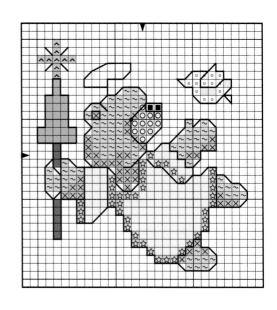

226

Design size: 21 wide x 22 high

Anchor	DMC
1	blanc
334	606
47	321
302	743
1031	3753
131	798
403	310

French Knots: 403
Backstitch:
227/701—sock & scarf stripes
351/400—arms
403—nose, mouth, buttons
236/3799—remaining outlines

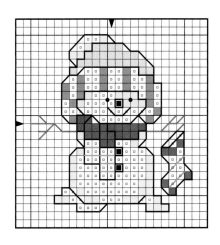

227

Design size: 35 wide x 28 high

Anchor	DMC
1	blanc
334	606
47	321
1031	3753
130	809
131	798
347	402
403	310

French Knots: 403
Backstitch:
334—collar stripes
351/400—hands
403—faces
236/3799—remaining outlines

228

Design size: 23 wide x 21 high

Anchor	DMC
1	blanc
302	743
225	702
186	959
131	798
97	554
403	310

French Knot: 403
Backstitch:
334/606—package ribbon
97—hat stripes
403—nose, mouth, bell
236/3799—remaining outline

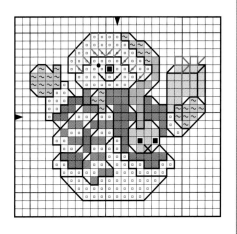

229

Design size: 25 wide x 29 high

	Anchor	DMC
▫	1	blanc
	36	3326
	334	606
	313	742
	1031	3753
~	121	809
	122	3807

French Knots: 236/3799
Backstitch:
47/321—lettering
236—remaining outlines

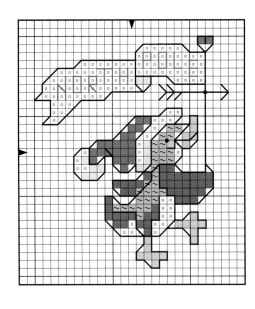

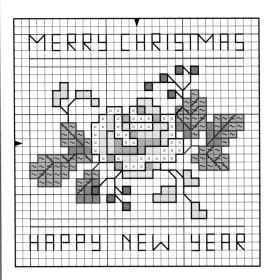

230

Design size: 28 wide x 27 high

	Anchor	DMC
▫	1	blanc
	73	963
	75	962
	334	606
	213	504
~	261	989
	267	469

Backstitch:
76/961—flower
334—red lines
20/815—berries, lettering
267—light green leaves & stems
246/986—dark green leaves &
    stems, green lines
374/420—berry stems

231

Design size: 28 wide x 29 high

	Anchor	DMC
▫	1	blanc
	334	606
~	1070	993
	1074	992
	1031	3753
	361	738

French Knots: 403/310
Backstitch:
131/798—motion lines
403—eyes, mouth
236/3799—remaining outlines

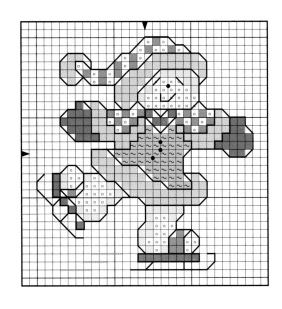

During this busy season, take a moment to relax and reflect.

232 Design size: 27 wide x 35 high

Anchor	DMC
~ 334	606
47	321
302	743
266	3347
246	986

Backstitch:
20/815—flowers, buds
1049/3826—cross
246—leaves, stems

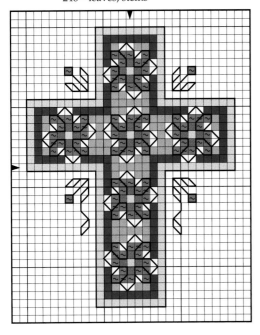

233 Design size: 27 wide x 22 high

Anchor	DMC	Backstitch:
∘ 1	blanc	1005/816—lines in red
334	606	candles
+ 47	321	308/781—flames
96	3609	228/700—branches,
△ 97	554	lines in green candles
301	744	236/3799—remaining
O 302	743	outlines
225	702	
◇ 227	701	
128	800	
130	809	

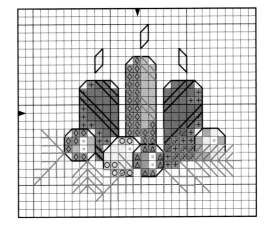

Playful rabbits in the holiday mood. You can't resist these
adorable bunnies, especially the one with mistletoe.

234

Design size: 32 wide x 22 high

Anchor	DMC
1	blanc
46	666
47	321
209	913
130	809
234	762
399	318

French Knots:
46—ornaments
302/743—ornaments
209—ornaments
109/209—ornaments
403/310—eyes, nose, buttons
Straight Stitch (scarf fringe): 209
Backstitch:
210/562—branch
403—nose
400/317—remaining outlines

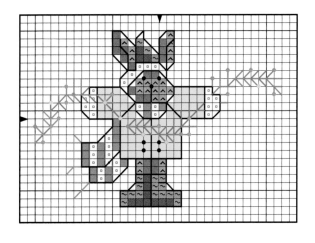

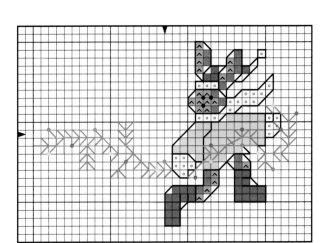

235

Design size: 34 wide x 23 high

Anchor	DMC
1	blanc
46	666
203	564
234	762
399	318

French Knots:
46—ornaments
302/743—ornaments
110/208—ornaments
403/310—eyes, nose
Backstitch:
210/562—branch
400/317—remaining outlines

236

Design size: 31 wide x 27 high

Anchor	DMC
1	blanc
47	321
225	702
234	762
399	318

French Knots:
47—ornaments
302/743—ornaments
109/209—ornaments
403/310—eyes, nose, buttons
Straight Stitch (scarf fringe): 131/798
Backstitch:
210/562—branch
131—scarf stripes
400/317—remaining outlines

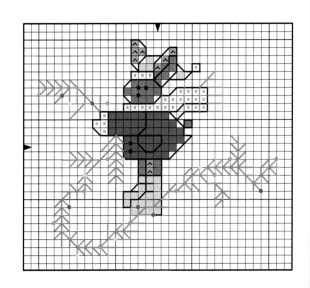

237

Design size: 30 wide x 34 high

Anchor	DMC
1	blanc
73	963
334	606
778	3774
311	3827
225	702
227	701
363	436
369	435
236	3799

French Knots: 236
Straight Stitch (scarf fringe): 227
Backstitch:
334—earmuff strap
236—remaining outlines

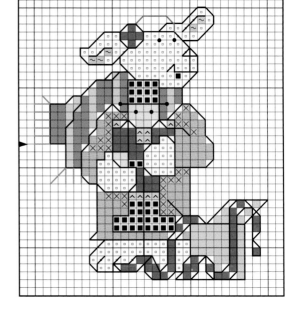

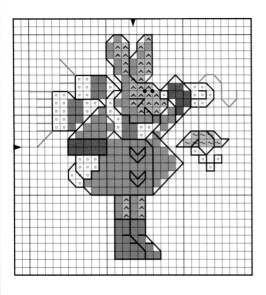

238

Design size: 27 wide x 28 high

Anchor	DMC
1	blanc
334	606
47	321
209	913
876	3816
234	762
399	318

French Knots: 403/310
Straight Stitch:
210/562—scarf fringe
403—whiskers
Backstitch:
1005/816—heart buttons
210—string
403—nose, mouth
400/317—remaining outlines

239

Design size: 34 wide x 29 high

Anchor	DMC
1	blanc
334	606
46	666
85	3609
361	738
368	437
225	702
227	701
398	415
235	414
236	3799

French Knots: 236
Straight Stitch (whiskers): 236
Backstitch:
46—candy canes
110/208—purple package & bow
236—remaining outlines

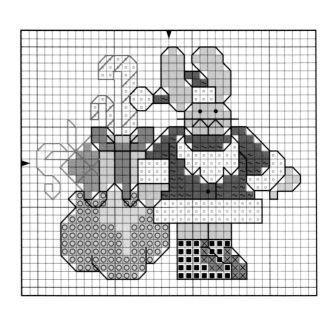

240

Design size: 30 wide x 24 high

Anchor	DMC
1	blanc
~ 46	666
47	321
311	3827
203	564
216	502
131	798
234	762
399	318
■ 403	310

French Knots: 403
Straight Stitch (scarf fringe): **210/562**
Backstitch: 400/317

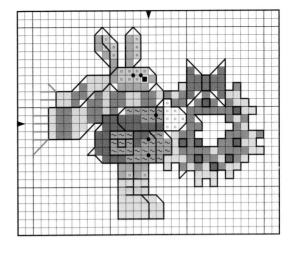

241

Design size: 34 wide x 32 high

Anchor	DMC
1	blanc
46	666
301	744
^ 313	742
216	502
1031	3753
131	798
372	738
△ 373	3828
~ 234	762
399	318
■ 403	310

French Knots: 403
Backstitch:
46—her scarf stripes, his scarf fringe
228/700—tree, her scarf fringe, his scarf stripes
131—snow
403—noses, mouths
236/3799—remaining outlines

242

Design size: 19 wide x 34 high

Anchor	DMC
1	blanc
334	606
301	744
302	743
227	701
1031	3753
234	762
■ 235	414

	Kreinik
gold #4 braid	202HL

French Knots: 236/3799
Straight Stitch (whiskers): 236
Backstitch:
47/321—bow
131/798—wings
gold #4 braid—halo
236—remaining outlines

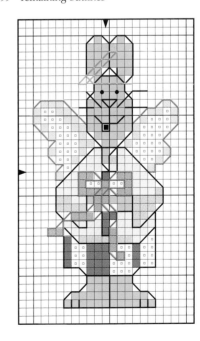

243

Design size: 32 wide x 16 high

	Anchor	DMC
	1	blanc
	334	606
	203	564
	128	800
	234	762

French Knots: 403/310
Straight Stitch (scarf fringe): 334
Backstitch:
334—stamp, lettering
209/913—return address, scarf stripes
403—mouth, tail
400/317—remaining outlines

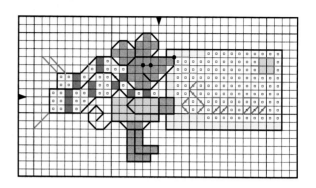

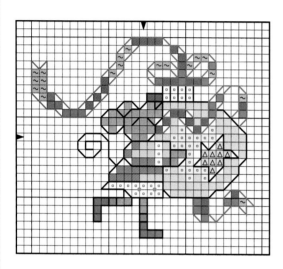

244

Design size: 29 wide x 25 high

	Anchor	DMC
	1	blanc
	334	606
	47	321
	328	3341
	301	744
	302	743
	305	726
	227	701
	130	809
	131	798
	234	762

French Knots: 227
Backstitch:
47—ribbon
236/3799—remaining outlines

245

Design size: 20 wide x 34 high

	Anchor	DMC
	1	blanc
	1020	3713
	311	3827
	240	966
	1031	3753
	131	798
	368	437

	Kreinik
gold #4 braid	202HL

French Knots: 236/3799
Straight Stitch (whiskers): 236
Backstitch:
gold #4 braid—halo
131—wings
236—remaining outlines

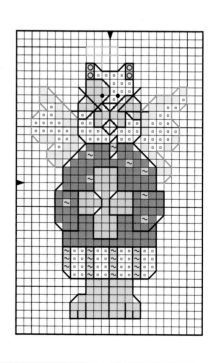

Santa untangles his string of lights and feeds the birds.

246

Design size: 29 wide x 34 high

	Anchor	DMC
▫	1	blanc
♡	36	3326
	334	606
+	47	321
	868	353
△	304	741
~	302	743
	241	966
	211	562
	1031	3753
	410	995
	236	3799

French Knots: 236
Backstitch:
211—light string
236—remaining outlines

247

Design size: 35 wide x 30 high

	Anchor	DMC
▫	1	blanc
⌃	36	3326
~	895	223
	334	606
	47	321
	4146	950
	225	702
	1031	3753
○	367	738
△	369	435
■	403	310

French Knots:
340/920—seeds
403—eyes
Backstitch:
340—nose, bag
403—buttons, lettering
236/3799—remaining outlines

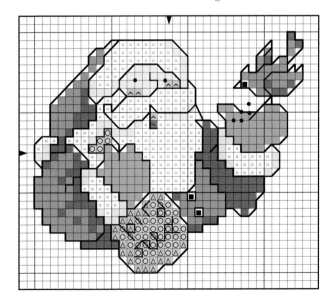

He's jolly, generous, and musical! This candy cane bordered
Santa sampler would bring a smile to Scrooge's face.

248

Design size: 33 wide x 31 high

	Anchor	DMC
▫	1	blanc
～	74	3354
▨	46	666
◉	47	321
▫	778	3774
∧	302	743
	240	966
▨	226	703
	128	800
△	129	809
	366	951
■	403	310

Backstitch:
355/975—nose, mouth, accordion pleats
403—eyes, mitten stripe ends
400/317—remaining outlines

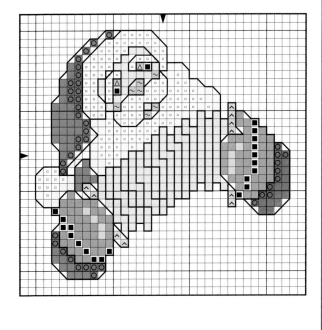

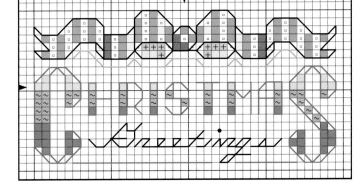

249

Design size: 39 wide x 19 high

	Anchor	DMC
▫	1	blanc
▨	334	606
▨	47	321
▫	305	743
+	306	783
▫	238	703
～	227	701
▨	211	562
▫	128	800

French Knot: 20/815
Backstitch:
20—ribbon, "Greetings"
1001/976—line under ribbon
211—bottom line, "CHRISTMAS" (use 1 strand next to cross stitches and 2 strands for letter extensions)

250

Design size: 27 wide x 29 high

	Anchor	DMC
▫	1	blanc
～	73	963
∧	74	3354
▨	46	666
	778	3774
×	362	437
+	347	402
	349	301
▨	400	317
■	403	310

French Knots: 403
Straight Stitch (cello strings): 400
Backstitch:
229/910—shirt stripes
349—skin
403 (2 strands)—eyes
400—remaining outlines

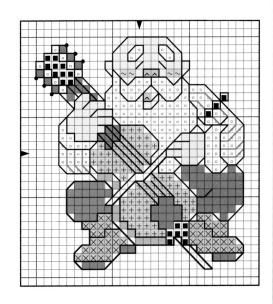

251

Design size: 21 wide x 32 high

	Anchor	DMC
▫	1	blanc
~	73	963
^	74	3354
■	46	666
□	778	3774
▨	311	3827
▨	378	841
▨	235	414
■	403	310

Backstitch:
46—shirt stripes
355/975—skin
403—belt
403 (2 strands)—eyes
400/317—remaining outlines

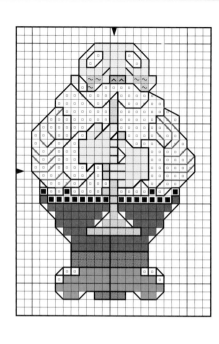

252

Design size: 25 wide x 29 high

	Anchor	DMC
▫	1	blanc
~	74	3354
■	46	666
□	778	3774
▨	228	700
+	347	402
▨	235	414
■	403	310

French Knots: 403
Straight Stitch (bow string): 403 (2 strands)
Backstitch:
228—sleeve stripes
403—belt, bow, violin slits & tuning pegs
403 (2 strands)—eyes
400/317—remaining outlines

253

Design size: 22 wide x 28 high

	Anchor	DMC
▫	1	blanc
■	46	666
⊙	47	321
□	778	3774
▨	302	743
□	128	800
▨	235	414
■	403	310

Backstitch:
355/975—horn, skin
403—eye, belt, boots
400/317—remaining outlines

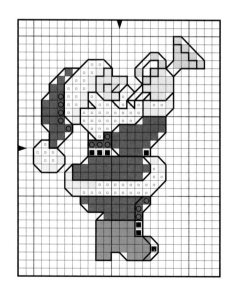

254

Design size: 26 wide x 28 high

	Anchor	DMC
▫	1	blanc
~	74	3354
■	46	666
□	778	3774
	891	676
□	128	800
	130	809
	399	318
✕	400	317
■	403	310

Backstitch: 403 (2 strands)
Backstitch:
46—shirt stripes
137/798—small drum vertical lines
355/975—skin, small drum stand, drum sticks
403—suspenders
400—remaining outlines

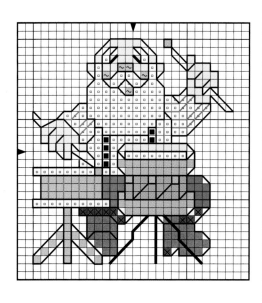

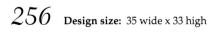

255

Design size: 29 wide x 30 high

	Anchor	DMC
▫	1	blanc
~	74	3354
■	46	666
□	778	3774
□	302	743
■	399	318
■	403	310

Backstitch:
46—triangle cord
137/798—shirt stripes
355/975—hands, triangle
403 (2 strands)—eyes
400/317—remaining outlines

256

Design size: 35 wide x 33 high

	Anchor	DMC
▫	1	blanc
	334	606
^	46	666
□	300	745
	362	437
△	369	435
	227	701
□	128	800
	398	415
	235	414
■	400	317

French Knots: 400
Straight Stitch (whiskers): 400
Backstitch:
146/798—paper, lettering
400—remaining outlines

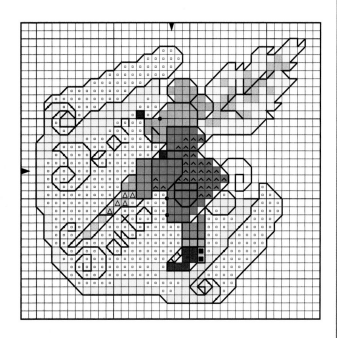

257

Design size: 28 wide x 29 high

	Anchor	DMC
□	1	blanc
+	36	3326
▨	334	606
▨	47	321
✕	1013	3778
~	361	738
∞	362	729
□	1031	3753
○	367	437
✳	369	435
▨	355	975
▫	398	415
■	403	310

Backstitch:
131/798—snow
403—boots, eye, nose
236/3799—remaining outlines

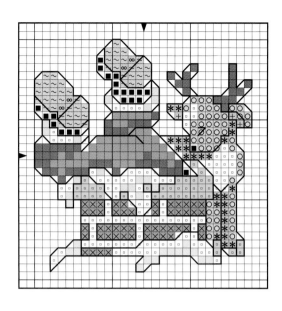

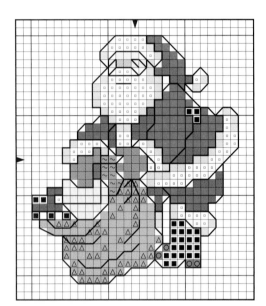

258

Design size: 27 wide x 31 high

	Anchor	DMC
□	1	blanc
▨	334	606
▨	47	321
□	4146	950
▨	868	353
□	301	744
▨	225	702
□	1031	3753
~	108	210
▨	110	208
▨	899	3782
△	393	640
○	400	317
■	403	310

Backstitch:
403—eyes, belt, boots, toy truck tires
236/3799—remaining outlines

259

Design size: 29 wide x 29 high

	Anchor	DMC
□	1	blanc
▨	334	606
□	4146	950
~	868	353
○	859	523
▨	861	520
△	920	932
▨	922	930
+	347	402
▨	1048	3776
■	403	310

French Knots:
334—line
403—eyes, hook
Backstitch:
334—line, hat flies
340/920—skin
403—eyebrows, pole, hook
236/3799—remaining outlines

260

Design size: 35 wide x 27 high

	Anchor	DMC
▫	1	blanc
■	334	606
△	47	321
~	4146	950
	313	742
	225	702
	1031	3753
	400	317
■	403	310

French Knots: 403
Backstitch:
334—reins
131/798—goose (except feet & beak)
340/920—feet & beak, Santa's nose
403—belt, boots
236/3799—remaining outlines

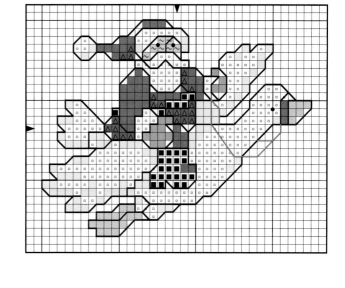

261

Design size: 27 wide x 30 high

	Anchor	DMC
▫	1	blanc
⊠	895	223
■	334	606
	47	321
~	4146	950
	306	783
	225	702
	130	809
⊙	131	798
	347	402
■	403	310

French Knots: 403
Backstitch:
340/920—skin
403—belt, buckle, boot tops
236/3799—remaining outlines

262

Design size: 34 wide x 32 high

	Anchor	DMC	Backstitch:
▫	1	blanc	334—red lights
	334	606	20/815—hat (except
△	47	321	fur trim)
	305	743	306—gold lights
⊙	306	783	246—leaves
~	242	989	845/730—cactus
■	246	986	130—blue lights
	842	3013	108—purple lights
◇	843	3012	235/414—fur trim on hat
	128	800	400/317—light cord
+	130	809	
	108	210	

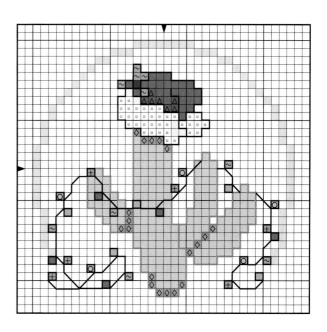

There's something for everyone in this holiday wreath
adorned with framed designs.

263

Design size: 28 wide x 27 high

Anchor	DMC
1	blanc
334	606
47	321
97	554
4146	950
868	353
306	783
158	747

French Knots: 403/310
Backstitch: 236/3799

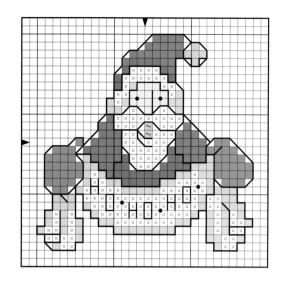

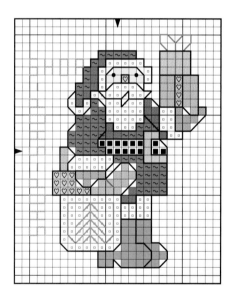

264

Design size: 23 wide x 29 high

Anchor	DMC
1	blanc
36	3326
334	606
47	321
868	353
306	783
241	966
130	809
235	414
403	310

French Knots: 403
Backstitch:
334—hyphens, bag handle & border,
   package bow, pant stripes
227/701—tree on bag
131/798—lettering
403—belt
236/3799—remaining outlines

265

Design size: 26 wide x 26 high

Anchor	DMC
1	blanc
885	739
334	606
238	703
227	701
367	738
369	435

French Knots: 403/310
Backstitch:
334—candy cane stripes
227—trees
351/400—bear (except mouth)
403—mouth
236/3799—remaining outlines

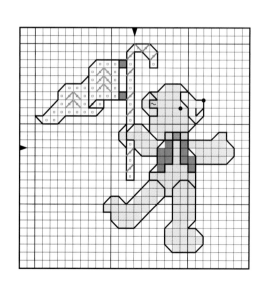

266

Design size: 9 wide x 29 high

	Anchor	DMC
□	1	blanc
■	334	606
■	47	321
□	4146	950
~	868	353
□	1031	3753

French Knots: 403/310
Backstitch:
131/798—beard, mustache
236/3799—hat, nose

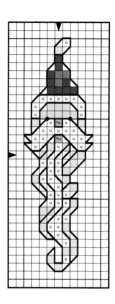

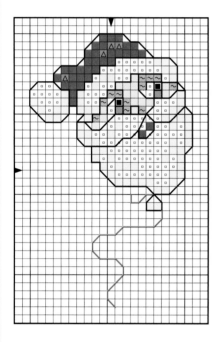

267

Design size: 21 wide x 34 high

	Anchor	DMC
□	1	blanc
■	334	606
□	4146	950
~	868	353
△	316	970
□	1031	3753
■	130	809
■	403	310

Backstitch:
334—string
403—eyes
236/3799—remaining outlines

268

Design size: 16 wide x 30 high

	Anchor	DMC
□	253	472
○	265	3347
✕	266	471
■	246	986

French Knots: 334/606
Backstitch:
334—ribbon
266—balls
246—leaves

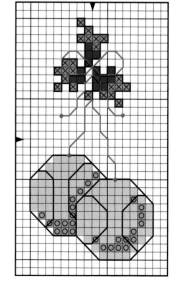

269

Design size: 18 wide x 31 high

Anchor	DMC
4146	950
882/883	758/3064
266	3347
246	986

French Knots: 334/606
Backstitch:
334—bow
246—leaves
358/801—ball

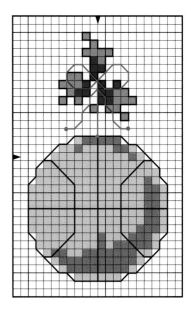

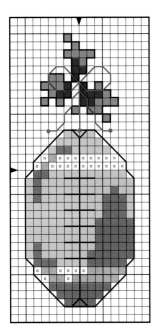

270

Design size: 14 wide x 34 high

Anchor	DMC
1	blanc
4146	950
882/883	758/3064
266	3347
246	986
234	762

French Knots: 334/606
Backstitch:
334—ribbon
246—leaves
358/801—ball

271

Design size: 18 wide x 31 high

Anchor	DMC
1	blanc
266	3347
246	986
234	762
235	414
403	310

French Knots: 334/606
Backstitch:
334—ribbon
246—leaves
403—ball

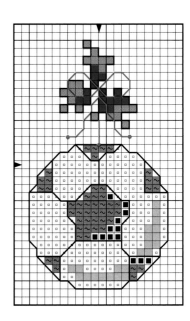

Candle wraps are easy to make with a bookmark and a ribbon tie.

272

Design size: 31 wide x 9 high

	Anchor	DMC
◌	1	blanc
■	46	666
▨	376	3774
▩	379	840

Backstitch:
229/910—lettering
137/798—lace
400/317—remaining outlines

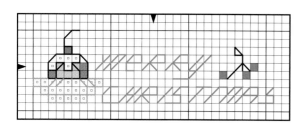

273

Design size: 33 wide x 15 high

	Anchor	DMC
■	334	606
▨	225	702
□	367	738
△	369	435
~	392	642
▨	393	640
■	403	310

French Knots: 403
Backstitch:
334—pull strings
228/700—tree (except trunk)
351/400—trunk, bear on right
403—wagon, nose, wheels, knob on string
236/3799—remaining outlines

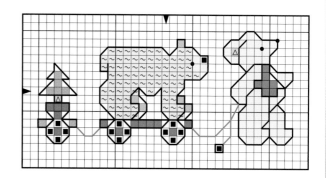

274

Design size: 17 wide x 17 high

	Anchor	DMC
▨	334	606
▨	238	703
□	367	738
~	369	435

French Knot: 403/310
Eyelet: 306/783
Backstitch:
228/700—tree (except trunk)
351/400—bear
236/3799—trunk, pot

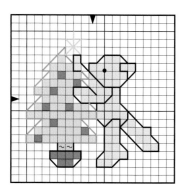

275

Design size: 50 wide x 20 high

	Anchor	DMC
◌	1	blanc
▨	334	606
□	367	738
~	369	435
▨	233	452
■	403	310

French Knots:
306/783—bells
403—eyes, noses
Backstitch:
403—nose
236/3799—remaining outlines

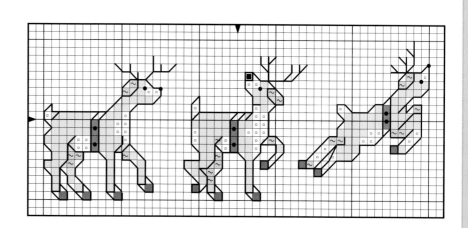

276

Design size: 35 wide x 31 high

	Anchor	DMC
▫	1	blanc
♡	73	963
+	40	956
▨	46	666
▫	1012	754
▫	240	966
~	226	703
▨	229	910
▫	1031	3753
△	130	809
▨	137	798
■	403	310

Backstitch:
403—eyes
401/413—remaining outlines

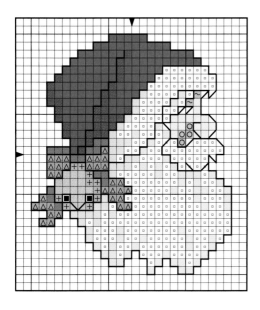

277

Design size: 26 wide x 30 high

	Anchor	DMC
▫	1	blanc
⊙	36	3326
▨	334	606
▨	47	321
▫	4146	950
~	868	353
▫	311	3827
+	307	783
△	238	703
▨	227	701
▫	1031	3753
■	403	310

Backstitch:
340/920—skin
403—eyes, inside bell
236/3799—remaining outlines

278

Design size: 35 wide x 33 high

	Anchor	DMC
▫	1	blanc
♡	36	3326
▨	334	606
▨	47	321
▫	4146	950
~	868	353
▫	1031	3753
▨	355	975
■	403	310

Backstitch:
355—skin
360/898—ball
403—eyes
236/3799—remaining outlines

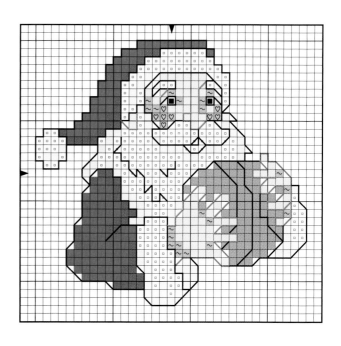

The fate of all snowmen is captured on a mini pillow with a ribbon hanger. Give a gift of joy with this handy tote.

279
Design size: 26 wide x 15 high

	Anchor	DMC
▫	1	blanc
~	334	606
	314	741
	238	703
	1031	3753
	400	317
■	403	310

Backstitch:
47/321—holly berries
228/700—holly leaves
131/798—snow
351/400—carrot
403—remaining outlines

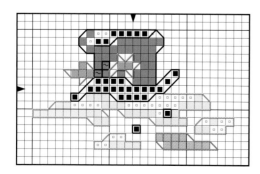

280
Design size: 35 wide x 22 high

	Anchor	DMC
▫	1	blanc
	334	606
O	311	3827
~	306	783
	238	703
	227	701
	128	800
	367	738
■	403	310

French Knots:
355/975—horn valves
403—nose, eye
Backstitch:
47/321—red lettering
306—halo
229/910—green lettering
131/798—gown
355—bear, horn
403—notes

Cute and amusing little animals celebrate the music of
the season in their own way, stitched into a colorful and
attractive sampler.

281

Design size: 33 wide x 35 high

	Anchor	DMC
▫	1	blanc
~	334	606
■	46	666
▫	300	745
∧	891	676
▫	240	966
◇	226	703
▪	229	910
▫	1047	402
▫	1048	3776
■	403	310

French Knots: 403
Straight Stitch (strings): 403
Backstitch:
20/815—berries
229—holly leaves
1048—paper scroll
403—remaining outlines

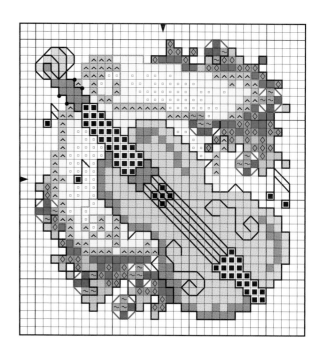

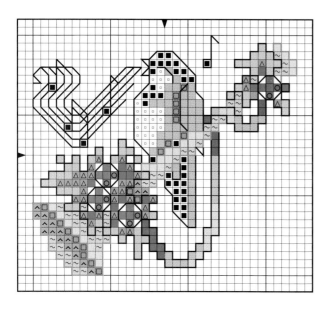

283

Design size: 35 wide x 35 high

	Anchor	DMC
▫	1	blanc
▫	50	605
▪	46	666
▪	20	815
~	226	703
▪	229	910
▫	130	809
▫	1047	402
▫	1048	3776
▫	398	415
▪	235	414
■	403	310

Backstitch: 403

282

Design size: 34 wide x 30 high

	Anchor	DMC		Anchor	DMC
▫	1	blanc	△	226	703
▫	49	3689	▪	229	910
▫	66	3688	▫	1047	402
▪	63	3804	▫	1048	3776
○	334	606	■	403	310
▪	46	666			
▫	305	743			
▫	303	742			
~	316	970			
∧	240	966			

Backstitch:
20/815—ribbon, berries
229—holly leaves
1048—horn
403—notes, staff, bird

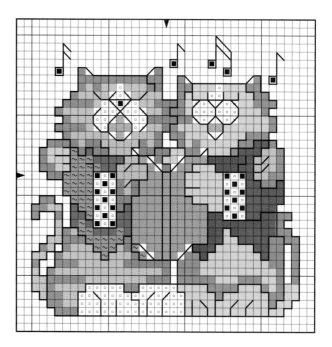

284 Design size: 35 wide x 32 high

	Anchor	DMC
▫	1	blanc
♡	50	605
	40	956
~	46	666
	20	815
	305	743
▫	303	742
	226	703
	398	415
◉	235	414
■	403	310

Backstitch:
20—berry, bow
326/720—harp
226—leaves
403—notes, mouse

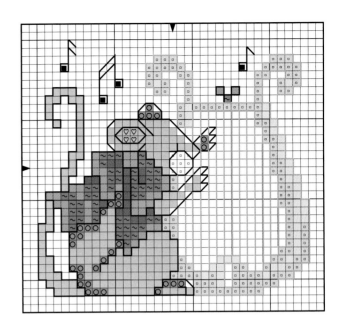

285 Design size: 34 wide x 34 high

	Anchor	DMC
▫	1	blanc
	46	666
	20	815
	303	742
	240	966
△	226	703
	137	798
	398	415
	235	414

French Knots: 403/310
Backstitch: 403

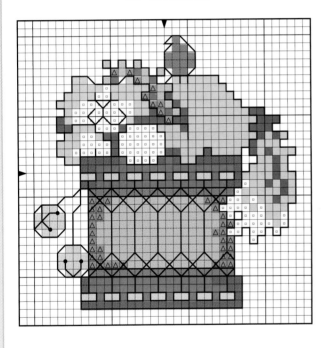

286 Design size: 34 wide x 33 high

	Anchor	DMC
▫	1	blanc
	40	956
~	334	606
	46	666
	20	815
	303	742
∧	316	970
◉	326	720
	240	966
△	226	703
	229	910
+	1047	402
▣	1048	3776
■	403	310

Backstitch:
20—bow, berries
229—holly leaves
351/400—bell outlines
403—notes, bird,
　　remaining bells

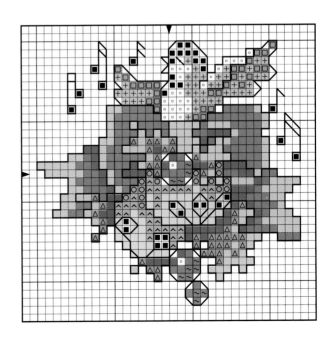

287

Design size: 35 wide x 31 high

	Anchor	DMC
□	1	blanc
	50	605
✕	40	956
	29	309
○	334	606
◇	46	666
	20	815
	305	743
∼	303	742
∼	316	970
	326	720
	240	966
△	226	703
	229	910
+	1047	402
∧	1048	3776
■	403	310

Backstitch:
20—berries, bow
229—holly leaves
351/400—horn
403—bird, notes

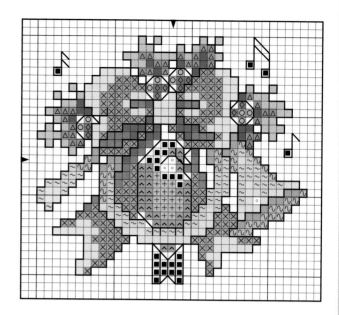

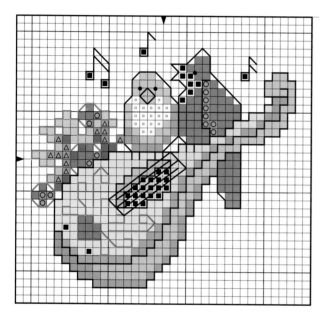

288

Design size: 34 wide x 32 high

	Anchor	DMC
□	1	blanc
○	334	606
	46	666
	20	815
	240	966
△	226	703
	229	910
	185	964
	187	958
	1047	402
	1048	3776
■	403	310

French Knots: 403
Straight Stitch
(strings): 403
Backstitch:
20/815—berries, heart
229—holly leaves,
decorative lines on
mandolin
403—remaining outlines

289

Design size: 35 wide x 35 high

	Anchor	DMC
□	1	blanc
○	50	605
	40	956
∧	46	666
∼	305	743
	303	742
	240	966
△	226	703
	1031	3753
■	403	310

Backstitch:
40—nose
20/815—pink & red, and striped dress edges
326/720—horn, halo
229/910—green dress edges
137/798—cat (except eyes & nose), wings
403—notes, staff, eyes

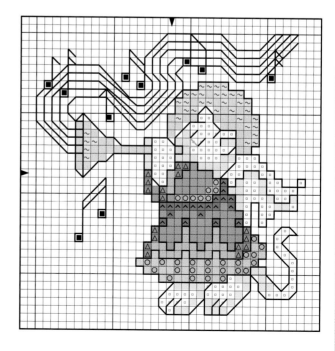

Christmas would not be complete without goodies from
the kitchen presented with goodies from your needle.

290

Design size: 33 wide x 34 high

Anchor	DMC
1	blanc
40	956
46	666
20	815
226	703
1031	3753
1047	402
1048	3776
403	310

French Knot: 20

Backstitch:
20—lettering
226—vines
403—eyes
401/413—remaining outlines

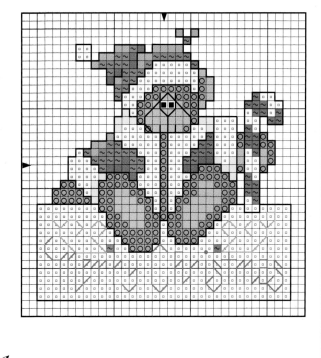

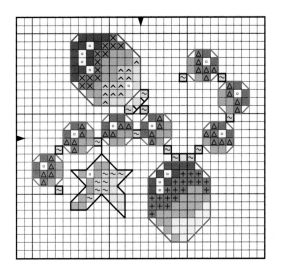

291

Design size: 28 wide x 26 high

Anchor	DMC		Anchor	DMC
1	blanc		879	500
334	606		128	800
46	666		130	809
20	815		142	798
305	743		139	797
303	742			
316	970	**Backstitch:**		
1043	369	20—red beads		
240	966	879—green light (except top)		
226	703	139—blue light (except top)		
229	910	340/920—star, light tops,		
		gold beads		

292

Design size: 33 wide x 35 high

Anchor	DMC
1	blanc
334	606
46	666
20	815
305	743
311	3827
226	703
229	910
1047	402
1048	3776

French Knot: 137/798

Backstitch:
1 (2 strands)—cherry highlights
20—cherries (except stems), red fruit bits
229—green fruit bits
137—lettering
1048—yellow fruit bits
381/938—fruitcake, stems

293

Design size: 30 wide x 30 high

	Anchor	DMC
▫	1	blanc
	334	606
~	47	321
	22	814
∧	314	741
	240	966
	226	703
	229	910
■	403	310

French Knot (2 strands): 1
Backstitch:
403—face, legs
401/413—remaining outlines

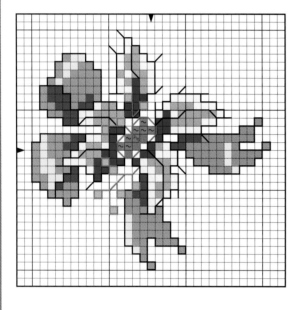

294

Design size: 31 wide x 30 high

	Anchor	DMC
~	334	606
	47	321
	329	3340
	300	745
	266	3347
	246	986
	128	800
	145	809
	147	797

Backstitch:
20/815—berries & stems
246—leaves
147—ribbon

295

Design size: 35 wide x 32 high

	Anchor	DMC
	333	608
−	19	304
	20	815
	8	3824
	305	743
~	306	783
∧	1001	976
	253	472
+	266	3347
	246	986
	206	564
⊠	205	912
	217	561
	128	800
△	129	809
	131	798

Backstitch:
20—red flowers, berries
1001—lettering (use 1 strand
     next to cross stitches
     and 2 strands for letter
     extensions)
246—yellow-green leaves,
     vines
217—blue-green leaves
131—blue flowers

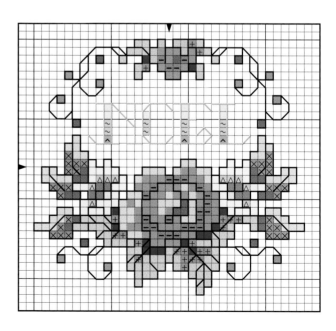

296

Design size: 28 wide x 26 high

Anchor	DMC
40	956
46	666
20	815
306	783
240	966
226	703
229	910
167	519
109	209

Backstitch:
229—wreath
403/310—remaining outlines

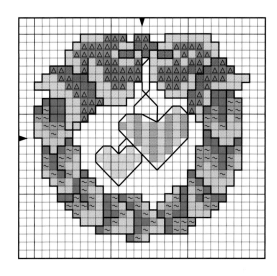

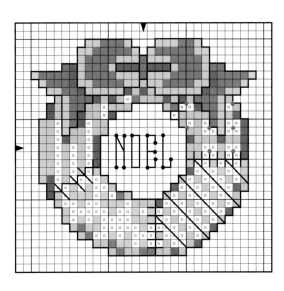

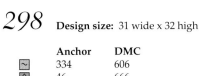

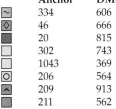

297

Design size: 29 wide x 27 high

Anchor	DMC
1	blanc
40	956
46	666
20	815
226	703
229	910
231	453

French Knots:
20—wreath berries
403/310—lettering
Backstitch:
20—bow, wreath stripes
403—remaining outlines

298

Design size: 31 wide x 32 high

Anchor	DMC
334	606
46	666
20	815
302	743
1043	369
206	564
209	913
211	562

Backstitch:
20—flowers
211—leaves, stems, vines

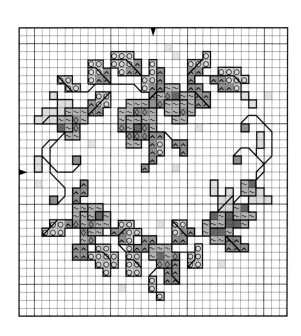

Spirited puppies and adorable kittens will take on
a life of their own on our sampler and perforated
plastic ornaments (page 159).

299

Design size: 26 wide x 26 high

	Anchor	DMC
□	1	blanc
	50	605
~	40	956
	46	666
	226	703
	128	800
	130	809
	1047	402

Backstitch: 403/310

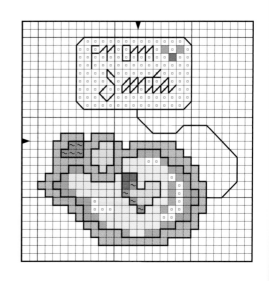

300

Design size: 23 wide x 33 high

	Anchor	DMC
□	1	blanc
	50	605
~	40	956
	46	666
	226	703
	128	800
	130	809
	1047	402

Backstitch: 403/310

301

Design size: 23 wide x 26 high

	Anchor	DMC
□	1	blanc
♡	36	3326
	334	606
	238	703
	227	701
	361	738
~	362	437
■	403	310

Backstitch:
334—bone string
355/975—dog (except eye & nose), bone
236/3799—scarf
403—eye, nose

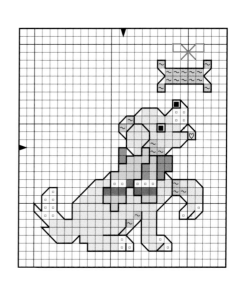

302

Design size: 23 wide x 26 high

	Anchor	DMC
▫	1	blanc
♡	36	3326
■	334	606
∧	47	321
~	313	742
■	1003	922
■	238	703

French Knots: 403/310
Backstitch:
334—mouse string
355/975—cat
236/3799—remaining outlines

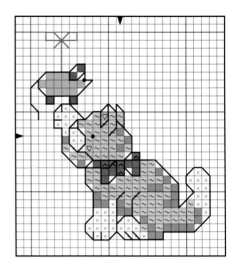

303

Design size: 25 wide x 28 high

	Anchor	DMC
▫	1	blanc
■	50	605
∧	334	606
■	47	321
■	238	703
□	1031	3753
△	933	543
○	347	402
■	403	310

French Knots: 403
Backstitch:
334—shirt stripes, bow
306/783—halo
229/910—wreath
131/798—wings
355/975—dog (except nose & mouth), bones
236/3799—remaining shirt
403—nose, mouth

304

Design size: 24 wide x 23 high

	Anchor	DMC
▫	1	blanc
■	36	3326
□	334	606
■	302	743
■	225	702
~	231	453
■	233	452

French Knot: 403/310
Straight Stitch (whiskers): 236/3799
Backstitch:
403—eyes, nose, mouth
236—remaining outlines

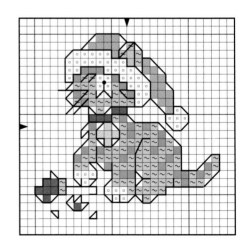

305

Design size: 23 wide x 29 high

	Anchor	DMC
▫	1	blanc
▨	334	606
▫	241	966
◇	226	703
▫	130	809
＋	131	798
▫	367	738
～	347	402
■	403	310

French Knot: 403
Backstitch:
46/666 (2 strands)—poles, skis
131—motion lines
403—eyebrow, nose
236/3799—remaining outlines

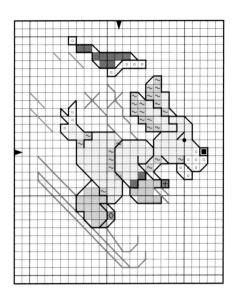

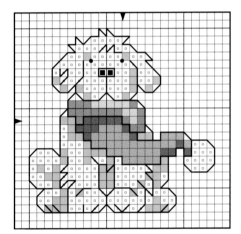

306

Design size: 24 wide x 23 high

	Anchor	DMC
▫	1	blanc
▫	334	606
▨	47	321
▫	238	703
▨	227	701
▫	234	762
■	403	310

French Knots: 403
Backstitch:
403—nose, mouth
236/3799—remaining outlines

307

Design size: 20 wide x 24 high

	Anchor	DMC
▫	1	blanc
～	36	3326
▨	334	606
▫	306	783
▫	1031	3753
▫	231	453
▨	233	452

French Knots: 403/310
Backstitch:
403—nose
236/3799—remaining outlines

308

Design size: 29 wide x 24 high

Anchor	DMC
1	blanc
334	606
47	321
241	966
226	703
130	809
131	798
367	738
347	402
403	310

French Knot: 403
Backstitch:
46/666—rope
131—motion lines
403—nose, eyebrow
236/3799—remaining outlines

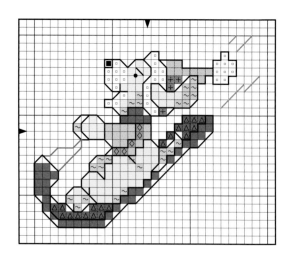

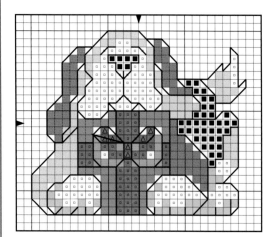

309

Design size: 28 wide x 23 high

Anchor	DMC
1	blanc
334	606
47	321
316	970
131	798
347	402
355	975
234	762
403	310

Backstitch:
236/3799—dog (except face), package
403—nose, mouth
403 (2 strands)—eyes

310

Design size: 18 wide x 24 high

Anchor	DMC
1	blanc
36	3326
334	606
238	703
1031	3753
361	738
362	437
403	310

French Knot: 403
Backstitch:
403—nose, mouth
236/3799—remaining outlines

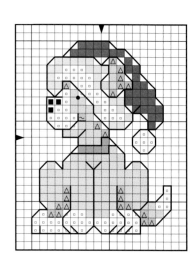

Towels, package ties, coaster, ornaments—they all add
up to a cheerful home and joyous Christmas.

311

Design size: 22 wide x 15 high

Anchor	DMC
334	606
302	743
241	966
361	738
362	437
236	3799

French Knot: 236
Backstitch: 236

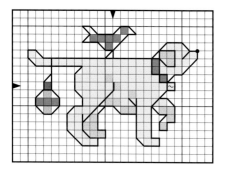

312

Design size: 25 wide x 16 high

Anchor	DMC
1	blanc
46	666
225	702
336	758

French Knots: 403/310
Backstitch:
229/910—branches
137/798—lettering
355/975—bear (except mouth & nose)
403—mouth
400/317—remaining outlines

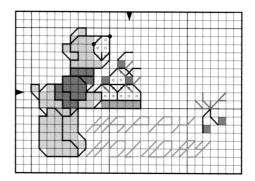

313

Design size: 35 wide x 14 high

Anchor	DMC
1	blanc
334	606
302	743
307	783
254	3348
129	809
96	3609
403	310

French Knots: 403
Backstitch:
20/815—red mitten
1049/3826—yellow mitten, bar
257/905—green mitten
131/798—blue mitten
99/552—purple mitten
403—lettering, hangers

314
Design size: 14 wide x 18 high

	Anchor	DMC
☐	36	3326
~	361	738
☒	306	783
⌃	369	435
☐	398	415
■	403	310

French Knots: 403
Straight Stitch (whiskers): 236/3799
Backstitch:
334/606—bow
355/975—buckle
236—mouse
403—boot

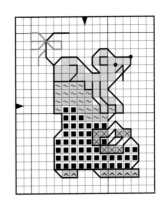

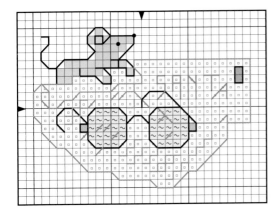

315
Design size: 28 wide x 20 high

	Anchor	DMC
▫	1	blanc
☐	36	3326
☐	891	676
☐	225	702
~	1031	3753
☐	398	415

French Knots: 403/310
Backstitch:
334/606—"Santa"
131/798—letter, envelope (except stamp), lens shine
351/400—glasses
236/3799—stamp, mouse

316
Design size: 27 wide x 14 high

	Anchor	DMC
▫	1	blanc
☐	36	3326
⌃	334	606
☐	47	321
☐	316	970
☐	227	701
~	1031	3753
☐	398	415

French Knots: 403/310
Backstitch: 236/3799

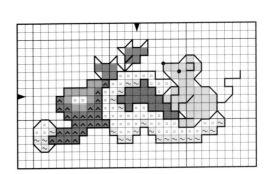

317

Design size: 31 wide x 35 high

	Anchor	DMC
▫	1	blanc
♡	36	3326
■	334	606
	86	3608
	306	783
	238	703
	1031	3753
	131	798
	347	402
	236	3799
■	403	310

French Knots: 403

Backstitch:
334—cord
131—white package stripes
355/975—rabbits (except noses & mouth)
403—noses & mouth, boots
403 (2 strands)—sled runners
236—remaining outlines

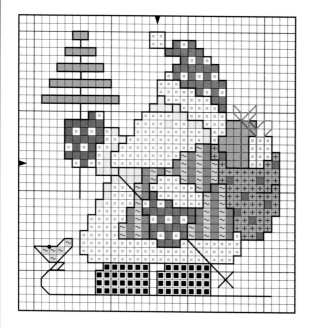

318

Design size: 32 wide x 33 high

	Anchor	DMC
▫	1	blanc
■	46	666
	1012	754
	226	703
	1031	3753
~	130	809
	137	798
+	98	553
■	403	310

French Knot: 401/413

Backstitch:
334/606—bows
403—boots, pole, ski
401—remaining outlines

With all the pre-made products available for Christmas, you
can quickly make a special gift for anyone.

319

Design size: 38 wide x 18 high

Anchor	DMC
1021	761
1024	3328
311	3827

French Knots: 1025/347
Backstitch:
1025—flower, lettering
210/562—branches

320

Design size: 26 wide x 30 high

Anchor	DMC
1	blanc
894	223
1027	3722
4146	950
891	676
1070	993
1031	3753
121	809
400	317

French Knot: 236/3799
Backstitch:
227/701—tree
340/920—Santa's face, bell
236—remaining outlines

321

Design size: 31 wide x 24 high

Anchor	DMC
334	606
46	666
316	970
305	743
303	742
240	966
226	703
229	910
130	809
142	798
139	797

French Knots: 1/blanc (2 strands)
Backstitch:
22/814—berries
229—leaves
139—candles
340/920—flames

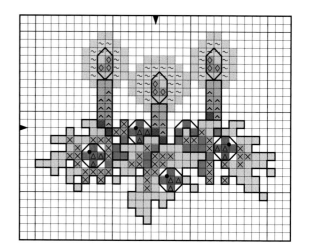

322

Design size: 28 wide x 27 high

Anchor	DMC
1	blanc
46	666
47	321
208	563
110	208

Backstitch:
46—candy cane
210/562—white ornaments, lettering
400/317—remaining outlines

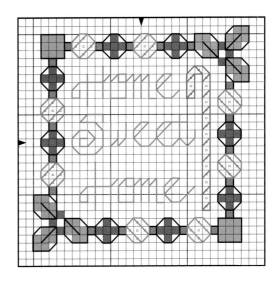

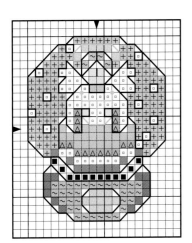

323

Design size: 18 wide x 23 high

Anchor	DMC
1	blanc
778	3774
302	743
185	964
129	809
131	798
108	210
1047	402
1049	3826
403	310

French Knots: 306/783
Backstitch:
306—halo, harp
131—glass
1049—wood base (except brass plate), angel
403—black base, brass plate

324

Design size: 29 wide x 22 high

Anchor	DMC
1	blanc
46	666
311	3827
313	742
301	744
253	472
266	3347
128	800
129	809
131	798
366	951
1047	402
1049	3826
403	310

Backstitch:
131—glass, cross, snow, church
  (except windows & door)
355/975—base
403—windows, door

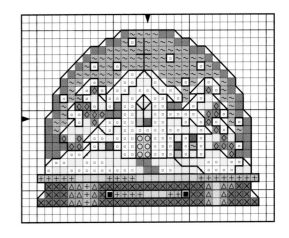

141

So real, you can almost smell the gingerbread baking.
These adorable gingerbread characters really make this
a charming sampler.

325

Design size: 32 wide x 30 high

Anchor	DMC
1	blanc
1094	604
334	606
240	966
1048	3776
351	400

French Knots:
1 (2 strands)—inner star tips
334—outer star tips
Backstitch: 1049/3826

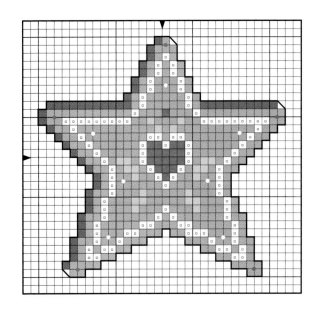

326

Design size: 29 wide x 35 high

Anchor	DMC
1	blanc
1094	604
66	3688
240	966
1048	3776
1049	3826
351	400

French Knots: 334/606
Backstitch:
334—cheeks, collar
351—mouth, hair, wrists

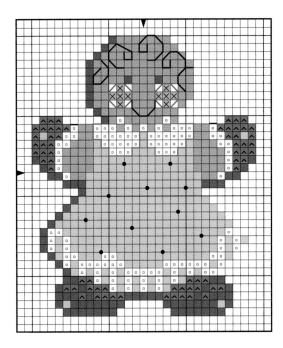

327

Design size: 29 wide x 35 high

Anchor	DMC
1	blanc
1094	604
66	3688
240	966
175	809
1048	3776
351	400

French Knots: 1 (2 strands)
Backstitch:
1 (4 strands)—hair
351—mouth, cheeks, wrists, ankles

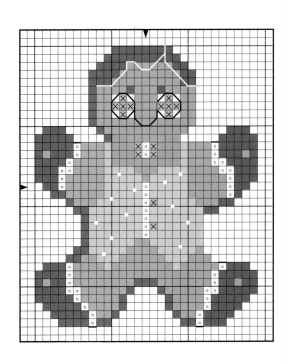

328

Design size: 30 wide x 35 high

Anchor	DMC
1	blanc
1094	604
334	606
240	966
108	210
1048	3776
351	400

Backstitch:
240—star, ornaments
1049/3826—remaining outlines

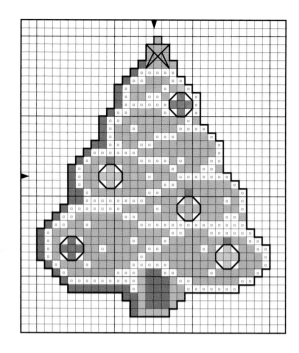

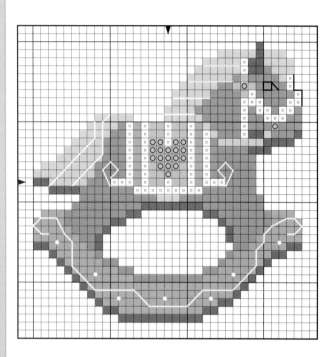

329

Design size: 35 wide x 35 high

Anchor	DMC
1	blanc
1094	604
66	3688
240	966
120	3747
1048	3776
351	400

French Knots: 1 (2 strands)
Backstitch:
1 (4 strands)—mane, tail, rocker, saddle
351 (2 strands)—eye
351—bridle

330

Design size: 34 wide x 33 high

Anchor	DMC
1	blanc
1094	604
334	606
86	3608
292	3078
240	966
108	210
1048	3776
1049	3826
351	400

French Knots: 240
Backstitch:
1 (4 strands)—heart outlines, post
    & chimney stripes
240—roof
240 (4 strands)—house curliques

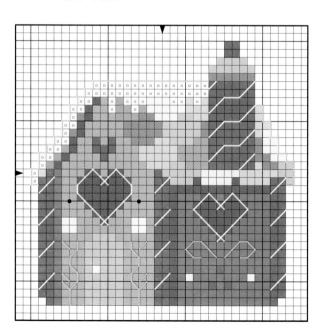

331

Design size: 35 wide x 33 high

	Anchor	DMC	Backstitch:
□	1	blanc	**46**—red frosting
	40	956	**20**—cherry
◉	334	606	**229**—green frosting, leaf
	46	666	**137**—blue frosting
	20	815	**371/434**—cookie
	240	966	**403/310**—stem
✕	226	703	
	229	910	
	128	800	
~	130	809	
	137	798	
	1047	402	

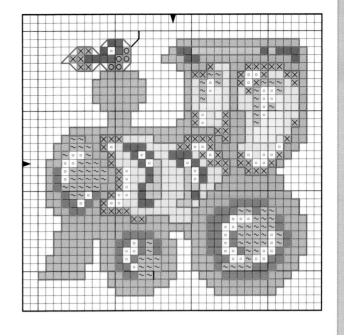

332

Design size: 29 wide x 32 high

	Anchor	DMC	Backstitch:
□	1	blanc	**46**—bow, berries
	50	605	**229/910**—leaves
◉	40	956	**187**—frosting
	46	666	**371/434**—cookie
	226	703	
	185	964	
	187	958	
	1047	402	
	1048	3776	

333

Design size: 33 wide x 35 high

	Anchor	DMC
□	1	blanc
	334	606
	1048	3776
	351	400

Backstitch:
351—heart outline
1 (2 strands)—remaining outlines

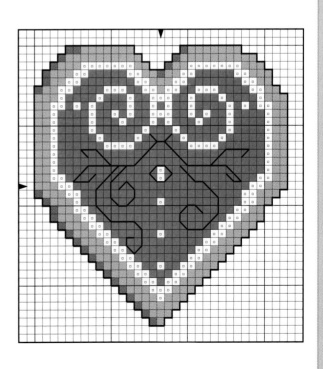

334

Design size: 32 wide x 33 high

	Anchor	DMC
▫	1	blanc
	305	743
~	303	742
	240	966
	226	703
	128	800
	130	809
	1047	402
■	403	310

Backstitch:
229/910—leaves
137/798—partridge (except eye)
403—eye
371/434—remaining cookie

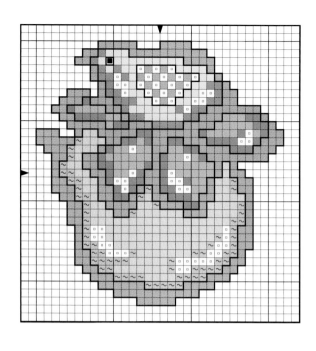

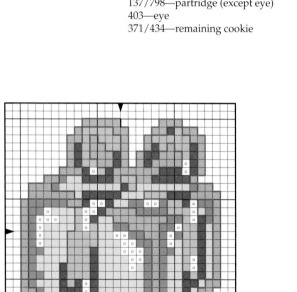

335

Design size: 26 wide x 28 high

	Anchor	DMC
▫	1	blanc
	40	956
	46	666
	240	966
	226	703
	1047	402

Backstitch:
20/815—ribbon
229/910—green package
371/434—remaining cookie

336

Design size: 31 wide x 29 high

	Anchor	DMC
▫	1	blanc
■	334	606
+	361	738
	4146	950
~	868	353
	241	966
	1031	3753
△	1033	932
■	403	310

Backstitch:
46/666—shirt stripes
340/920—hands
403—eyes
236/3799—remaining outlines

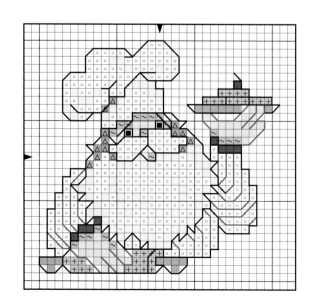

337
Design size: 34 wide x 11 high

	Anchor	DMC
	1	blanc
	227	701
	1008	3773
✕	1007	3772

French Knots: 400/317
Backstitch:
46/666—candy canes
227—cup rims & handles
400—remaining outlines

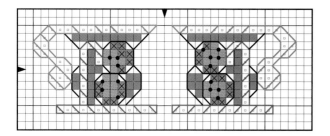

338
Design size: 26 wide x 11 high

	Anchor	DMC
	1	blanc
	46	666
	86	3608
	226	703
	361	738

Backstitch:
46—house eaves, candy cane stripes
371/434—roof shingles
400/317—remaining outlines

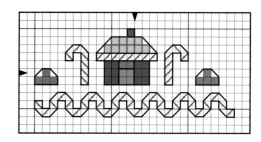

339
Design size: 32 wide x 26 high

	Anchor	DMC
	1	blanc
	46	666
	86	3608
	301	744
~	302	743
	227	701
	1008	3773
✕	1007	3772

French Knots: 400/317
Backstitch:
46—candy canes
400—remaining outlines

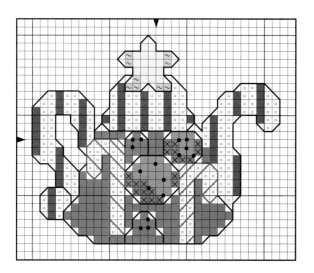

340
Design size: 28 wide x 26 high

	Anchor	DMC
	1	blanc
	36	3326
	334	606
	225	702
	367	738
△	369	435
■	403	310

French Knots: 403
Backstitch:
334—hat stripes
47/321—lettering
351/400—dog (except face)
236/3799—hat, tongue
403—remaining face, pawprints

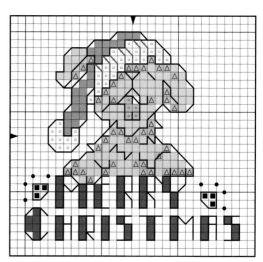

Santa and his helpers join you to make gift giving extra special.

341

Design size: 27 wide x 30 high

	Anchor	DMC
□	1	blanc
▨	334	606
✚	47	321
□	306	783
□	241	966
◇	226	703
□	1010	951
～	367	738
◎	347	402
△	1047	3776
▨	850	926
■	403	310

French Knots: 403
Backstitch:
46/666—sack bow
403—nose, belt
236/3799—remaining outlines

342

Design size: 18 wide x 30 high

	Anchor	DMC
□	1	blanc
□	74	3354
▨	46	666
□	368	437
▨	371	434
□	234	762
▨	235	414
■	403	310

French Knot: 403
Backstitch:
229/910—tree
371—reindeer (except inner ear line & nose), antlers
403—notes, nose
400/317—remaining outlines

343

Design size: 33 wide x 27 high

	Anchor	DMC
□	1	blanc
～	36	3326
▨	334	606
▨	47	321
□	4146	950
□	868	353
□	301	744
□	227	701
□	1031	3753
▨	131	798

French Knots: 334 (2 strands)
Backstitch:
334 (2 strands)—frame stripes
228/700—holly leaves
131—lettering
236/3799—remaining outlines

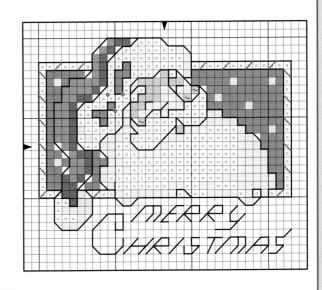

344

Design size: 24 wide x 26 high

	Anchor	DMC
▫	1	blanc
■	334	606
△	46	666
■	20	815
▫	240	966
✕	226	703
▨	229	910
■	403	310

Backstitch: 403

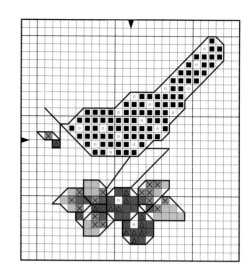

345

Design size: 32 wide x 34 high

	Anchor	DMC
▫	1	blanc
♡	36	3326
■	334	606
~	868	353
▫	347	402
▨	238	703
▫	1031	3753
▨	130	809
+	1008	3773
▨	1007	3772
■	403	310

Backstitch:
340/920—skin, rope
403—eye, eyelid, hat trim
236/3799—remaining outlines

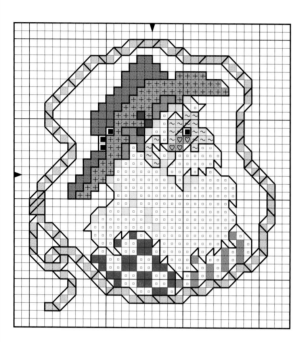

346

Design size: 27 wide x 33 high

	Anchor	DMC
▫	1	blanc
▨	36	3326
■	334	606
▨	225	702
▫	1031	3753
▫	361	738
~	362	437
▨	899	3782
■	403	310

French Knots: 334 (2 strands)
Backstitch:
228/700—holly leaves
351/400—bear (except eyes, nose, mouth)
236/3799—hat, vest
403—eyes, nose, mouth, buttons

347

Design size: 29 wide x 30 high
Note: Add Mill Hill Glass Treasure green
leaves 12197 to top of package.

	Anchor	DMC
□	1	blanc
▨	334	606
▨	238	703
▨	231	453
~	233	452
■	403	310

Backstitch:
403—eyes, nose, muzzle
236/3799—remaining outlines

348

Design size: 26 wide x 31 high
Note: Add Mill Hill Glass Treasure
snowflake 12035 to top of package.

	Anchor	DMC
□	1	blanc
♡	36	3326
■	334	606
▨	225	702
△	130	809
▨	131	798
○	85	3609
▨	87	3607
▨	367	738
~	369	435
■	403	310

Backstitch:
403—eyes, nose, mouth
236/3799—remaining outlines

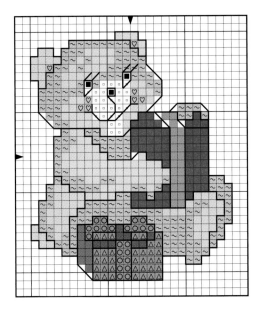

349

Design size: 34 wide x 32 high

	Anchor	DMC
□	1	blanc
♡	36	3326
■	334	606
⌃	314	741
+	301	744
○	302	743
~	1031	3753
▨	130	809
▨	367	738
△	369	435
■	403	310

Backstitch:
46/666—shirt stripes
355/975—holder, candle, flame, glow
236/3799—bear (except eyes, nose, mouth),
    clothes, book
403—eyes, nose, mouth

These holiday greetings keep on saying, "Happy Holidays!", while snow globes brighten the gloomiest winter day.

350

Design size: 27 wide x 25 high

	Anchor	DMC
□	1	blanc
	334	606
△	46	666
	20	815
	240	966
	226	703
	128	800
~	130	809
	142	798
■	403	310

Backstitch:
46—lettering
22/814—cherry
229/910—leaves
139/797—ribbon
403—remaining outlines

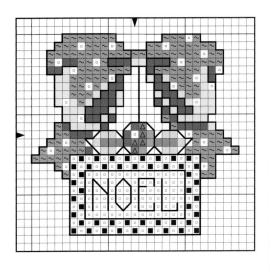

351

Design size: 31 wide x 35 high

	Anchor	DMC
□	1	blanc
	334	606
	311	3827
∧	1002	977
	1048	3776
△	376	3774
○	1084	840
■	1086	839

French Knot: 1086
Backstitch:
334—ribbon
1049/3826—bell (except top)
1086—bell top, lettering

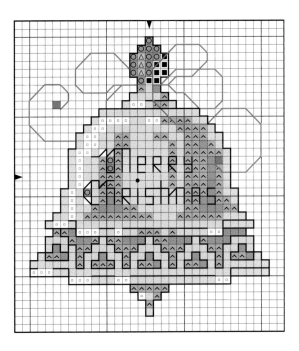

352

Design size: 31 wide x 30 high

	Anchor	DMC
□	1	blanc
△	334	606
	47	321
	254	3348
◇	258	905
	246	986
	234	762
○	399	318
	235	414
■	236	3799

Backstitch:
20/815—ribbon, berries
236—bells

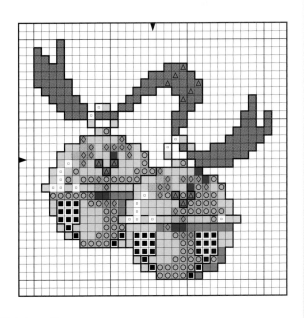

355

Design size: 27 wide x 34 high

	Anchor	DMC		Anchor	DMC
□	1	blanc		109	209
~	334	606		1047	402
	46	666	△	1048	3776
○	303	742		1049	3826
	259	772	**Backstitch:**		
◇	240	966	20/815—berries		
	226	703	229/910—tree (except trunk),		
^	1031	3753	base leaves		
	128	800	132/797—snow, glass		
	130	809	1049—tree trunk, base		

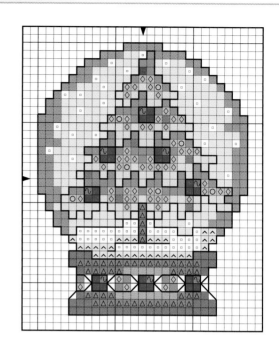

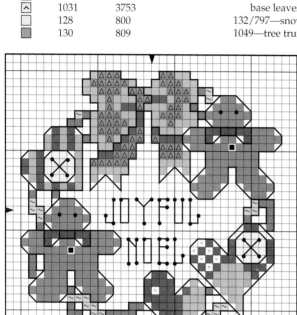

354

Design size: 34 wide x 35 high

	Anchor	DMC		Anchor	DMC
□	1	blanc		374	420
	40	956	■	403	310
	46	666	**French Knots:** 403		
	20	815	**Backstitch:**		
	301	744	20—hearts, red bows		
	240	966	229—green bow		
△	226	703	351/400—wreath,		
	229	910	gingerbread men		
	1048	3776	403 (2 strands)—lettering		
~	373	3828	403—remaining outlines		

353

Design size: 28 wide x 34 high

	Anchor	DMC	**French Knots:**	
□	1	blanc	334—berries	
	334	606	403—eyes, tuning pegs	
	47	321	**Backstitch:**	
	238	703	306/783—halo	
	1031	3753	229/910—leaves	
	367	738	131/798—wings	
^	369	435	355/975—bear (except nose)	
■	403	310	236/3799—gown	
			403—mandolin, nose	

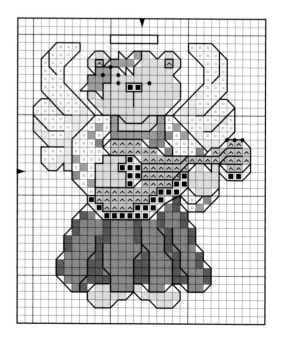

356

Design size: 39 wide x 6 high

	Anchor	DMC		Anchor	DMC
□	305	743	~	241	966
	307	783		227	701
	1043	369	**Backstitch:** 227		

357
Design size: 16 wide x 33 high

Anchor	DMC
1	blanc
334	606
46	666
778	3774
6	754
301	744
891	676
130	809
146	798
400	317
403	310

Backstitch:
46—mouth
403—remaining outlines

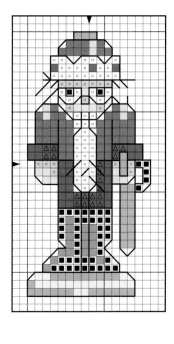

358
Design size: 15 wide x 34 high

Anchor	DMC
1	blanc
334	606
46	666
778	3774
6	754
301	744
891	676
130	809
146	798
400	317
403	310

French Knots: 403
Backstitch:
46—mouth
403—remaining outlines

359
Design size: 17 wide x 35 high

Anchor	DMC
1	blanc
778	3774
6	754
8	3824
891	676
225	702
229	910
235	414
403	310

Backstitch:
46/666—feather (except stem), mouth
229/910—feather stem
403—remaining outlines

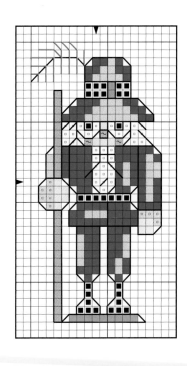

Display your treats by accenting with quick-to-stitch designs.

360
Design size: 30 wide x 24 high

	Anchor	DMC
~	46	666
	47	321
	301	744
+	302	743

French Knots: 137/798
Backstitch:
228/700—branches
236/3799—horn, ribbon

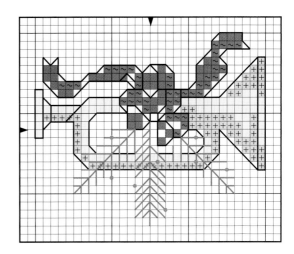

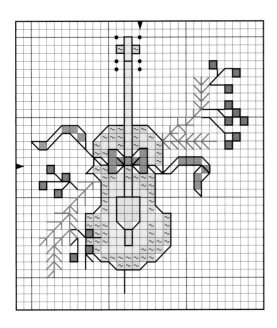

361
Design size: 28 wide x 32 high

	Anchor	DMC
	46	666
	311	3827
	136	799
	366	951
~	368	437

French Knots: 236/3799
Backstitch:
228/700—branches
137/798—ribbon
236—remaining outlines

362
Design size: 20 wide x 33 high

	Anchor	DMC
	46	666
	386	3823
~	301	744
	891	676
	215	320
	110	208

French Knots: 236/3799
Backstitch: 236

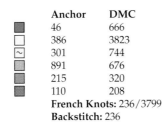

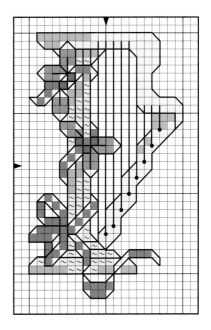

363

Design size: 35 wide x 29 high

	Anchor	DMC
□	1	blanc
△	46	666
▨	1006	304
~	361	738
⬙	362	437
+	373	3828
	254	3348
	227	701
◉	229	910
	109	209
^	1047	402
✕	1048	3776
	936	632

French Knots: 403/310
Backstitch:
46—sleeves
1005/816—mouth, berries
373—basket
229—leaves
1049/3826—remaining outlines

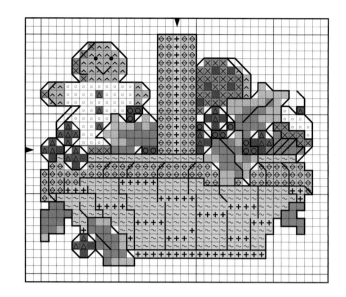

364

Design size: 35 wide x 36 high

	Anchor	DMC
□	1	blanc
	329	3340
□	300	745
◯	293	727
^	891	676
	890	729
	266	3347
	246	986
	881	945
	883	3064
■	358	801

Backstitch:
329—flame
890—candle
358—pine cones
401/413—lettering

365

Design size: 39 wide x 55 high

	Anchor	DMC
	334	606
□	302	743
	254	3348
~	266	3347
	210	562

Backstitch: 210

HOLIDAY GREETINGS

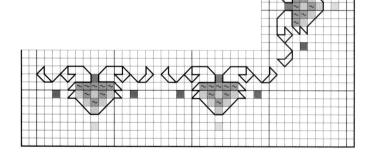

FABRICS, NEEDLES, AND THREADS

Some of these designs were cross stitched on 16-count Aida cloth with two strands of floss. Some designs were stitched on 14-count fabric, vinyl, or perforated plastic or paper. On 14-count fabrics, two strands of floss are usually used. On 14-count vinyl or perforated surfaces, three strands are recommended because the area over which each stitch is made is relatively small. On 18-count fabrics, use one strand of floss.

Use a blunt-tipped tapestry needle, size 24 or 26, for most stitching. The higher the number the smaller the needle. The most commonly used thread for counted cross stitch is six-strand cotton embroidery floss. Divide it into individual strands, then put the required number back together before threading the needle.

Our photographed models were stitched with Anchor embroidery floss and the DMC floss numbers are also listed. The companies have different color ranges, so these are only suggested color substitutions. A "blended" color is noted in the color key as two numbers separated by a slash; use one strand of each floss color. If a color is used for a specialty stitch but not a cross stitch, the color numbers are listed (Anchor is first) separated by a slash mark.

WORKING FROM CHARTED DESIGNS

Each square on a chart corresponds to a space for a cross stitch on the stitching surface. The color in a square shows the floss color to be used for the stitch. The chart colors are not necessarily close matches for the actual floss colors. They have been charted to provide contrast for ease in reading the charts. Often a symbol has been added to the color square to provide even more contrast. The chart is accompanied by a color key which lists the numbers of the floss colors to be used. The design stitch width and height are given; centers are shown by arrows.

Straight lines over or between squares indicate backstitches or straight stitches. Eyelets are shown by their shapes, and French knots by dots. Occasionally color is used for lines and dots to help differentiate the colors to be used. For other charts, a thicker line is used for further clarification.

GETTING STARTED

To begin in an unstitched area, bring threaded needle to front of fabric. Hold an inch of the end against the back, then anchor it with your first few stitches. To end threads and begin new ones next to existing stitches, weave through the backs of several stitches.

THE STITCHES

Cross Stitch

The cross stitch is formed in two motions. Follow the numbering in **Fig 1** and bring needle up at 1, down at 2, up at 3, down at 4, to complete the stitch. Work horizontal rows of stitches, **Fig 2**, wherever possible. Bring thread up at 1, work half of each stitch across the row, then complete the stitches on your return.

Fig 1

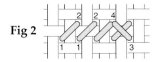
Fig 2

Backstitch

Backstitches are worked after cross stitches have been completed. They may slope in any direction and are occasionally worked over more than one square of fabric. **Fig 3** shows the progression of several stitches; bring thread up at odd numbers and down at even numbers.

Frequently you must choose where to end one backstitch color and begin the next color. Choose the object that should appear closest to you. Backstitch around that shape with the appropriate color, then backstitch the areas behind it with adjacent color(s). Occasionally, a color key will have two backstitch symbols (a thick line and a thin one), or colored lines to help you differentiate colors.

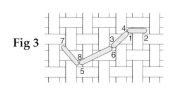
Fig 3

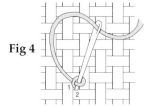
Fig 4

French Knot

Bring thread up where indicated on chart. Wrap floss once around needle, **Fig 4**, and reinsert needle at 2, close to 1, but at least one fabric thread away from it. Hold wrapping thread tightly and pull needle through, letting thread go just as knot is formed. For a larger knot, use more strands of floss, but wrap only once. Occasionally, the color key will use colored dots to help differentiate the floss colors to be used.

Eyelet

This is a technique that produces a starburst effect. Bring thread up at any point along the outside of the charted shape, **Fig 5**, and stitch down into the center. Continue to work around the shape as shown on the chart, always entering at center of eyelet. Occasionally, the color key will use colored lines to help differentiate the floss colors.

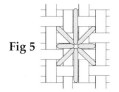
Fig 5

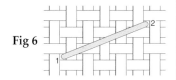
Fig 6

Straight Stitch

A straight stitch, **Fig 6**, is made like a long backstitch. Come up at one end of the stitch and down at the other. Follow the chart for exact placement. Occasionally, the color key will use colored lines to help differentiate the floss colors.

FINISHING NEEDLEWORK

Wash stitched fabric in cool water with a gentle soap. Rinse well. Roll in a towel and squeeze out excess moisture. Place face down on a dry towel and iron carefully. Frame or finish as desired.

To make perforated plastic or paper ornaments or package ties, stitch the design, then cut excess at least one space beyond all stitches. Glue one or two larger pieces of felt to the wrong side with a hanging loop sandwiched in between, then trim felt edges as desired.

For bell pulls, use purchased hangers. Sew the side edges of the fabric to make a sleeve, then fold top and bottom edges over hangers and secure in place. Trim as desired.

Design Index

This index will help you locate designs by subject matter. Numbers refer to the design's page number.

Product Sources

Please check your local craft or needlework shop for the materials and pre-made products you may wish to use. If you are unable to find a particular item, please contact the manufacturers and distributors listed here.

Country Wire (1-770-458-6500):
wire hangers

Charles Craft (1-800-277-0980):
waste canvas, jar lids, and bookmarks

Crafter's Pride (1-800-277-6850):
snowglobes, mini snowglobes, bottle bags, gift bags, mugs, sipper cups, can holders, towels, table linens, napkin rings, address book, memo book, photo album, stocking, mini pillows, snowflakes, gift tags, bibs, baby bottle warmer, bookmarks, and potholders

Yarn Tree (1-800-247-3952):
perforated paper and plastic, acrylic coasters, oval charms, and greeting cards

Westex Corp. (1-908-624-0093):
small goldtone frames